The Great

RIBS

Book

The Great

RIBS

Book

Hugh Carpenter & Teri Sandison

Food Styling by Carol Cole

TEN SPEED PRESS

Berkeley, California

To family and friends
united around a feast of ribs.

Copyright © 1999 by Hugh Carpenter and Teri Sandison
Photographs © 1999 by Teri Sandison

Ten Speed Press
P.O. Box 7123
Berkeley, California 94707
www.tenspeed.com

Distributed in Australia by Simon and Schuster Australia, in Canada by
Ten Speed Press Canada, in New Zealand by Southern Publishers Group,
in South Africa by Real Books, and in the United Kingdom and Europe by
Airlift Book Company.

Cover and book design by Beverly Wilson
Typography by Laurie Harty

Library of Congress Cataloging-in-Publication Data on file
with the publisher.

ISBN 1-58008-071-5

First printing, 1999
Printed in China

10 11 12 13 14 15 — 08 07 06 05

Contents

Introduction
6

Great Ribs of All Types
9

Preparation and Cooking Techniques
17

Show-Stopping Asian Ribs
35

New Approaches for American Ribs
57

Mexican and Southwestern Masterpieces
79

Mediterranean and Caribbean Ribs
95

Fruit-Based Barbecue Glazes
113

Succulent Braised Ribs
133

Artists' Credits
150
Acknowledgments
150
Conversion Charts
151
Glossary
152
Index
156

Introduction

Rib lovers are everywhere. Many of us remember ribs from childhood, mounded on platters at family picnics, roadside rib shacks, and church suppers. And every rib connoisseur knows an ideal cooking method, a secret blend of seasonings, a type of hardwood chips that generates the perfect smoky aroma, and where to find the best rib joint in the area.

This book is for rib connoisseurs. But it's also for the occasional backyard cook and for first-time cooks ready to begin a lifetime of pleasure cooking ribs.

Few other smells are as welcoming as the smell of ribs slowly cooking on the grill, roasting in the oven, or bubbling in a delectable sauce. You'll find that dinner guests move without invitation toward the cooking ribs, and usually won't stop eating ribs until just a pile of bones remains. Sharing a platter of ribs is a great way to reaffirm old friendships or to get new ones off to a great start.

The following recipes take only minutes to prepare. Most of the rubs and marinades can be made days in advance. Except for an occasional ethnic product, all the ingredients are available at most supermarkets. Or, if you are pressed for time, follow the fail-safe cooking instructions outlined in chapter 2, and use a commercial barbecue sauce.

When cooking these recipes, remember that "low and slow" is best. Rib meat is tough. It requires low heat and long cooking to break down the meat fiber, render the fat, and make the meat succulent and tender.

Every recipe specifies a type of rib, but feel free to substitute your favorite. All the common varieties are described in the next section. Our personal preference, whether smoking, grilling, roasting, or simmering ribs in liquid, is the king of ribs, pork baby back ribs.

All the recipes in this book yield enough for the ribs to be served as entrées for four. They can also be served as appetizers for six to ten, or you can double or triple them to serve larger groups. When serving ribs as an entrée, accompany them with other simple dishes such as garden salads, an easy side dish like garlic bread or roasted potatoes, and for dessert, ice creams, cobblers, and pies.

We hope you have the same pleasure cooking and serving these ribs as we have had creating these recipes at our home. Gather your family and friends, open some icy drinks, cook generous amounts of ribs, and enjoy the pleasure of all those gathered as they relish one of the world's most satisfying foods.

Hugh Carpenter and Teri Sandison

Great Ribs of All Types

Spareribs

The word *spareribs* always refers to ribs from pigs (the word is never used for beef or lamb) and, specifically, to the side or underbelly of the pig. Most markets sell these "sides" or "slabs" with the fatty, cartilage brisket end that runs across the top quarter of each side of spareribs. Ask the butcher to trim off the brisket end or complete this as shown in the photograph. We freeze these scraps and add them to the pot when making "chicken stock."

The flap of meat that extends partway across the side of ribs is called the skirt. Most ribs sold in supermarkets will have the skirt removed—these are sometimes called "St. Louis–style ribs." Ribs with the skirt left on—"Kansas City–style"—are more often bought fresh from a butcher. Whether or not to remove the skirt is a matter of personal preference. When cooked, it will become as tender as the rest of the meat. Spareribs are great smoked, grilled, roasted, or braised.

Serving portion:

As an appetizer, 2 ribs per person. As an entrée, $^1/_2$ side of ribs per person.

Kansas City–Style

St. Louis–Style

Pork Baby Back Ribs

Cut from the loin or back section, pork baby back ribs are the Rolls-Royce of ribs. With more meat and less fat than most ribs, baby backs are great smoked, grilled, roasted, or braised. Just a few years ago, pork baby back ribs were mostly sold by Asian markets, but now they are available at many supermarkets. Since the quality ranges from frozen ribs with little meat to fresh pork baby back ribs containing plenty of succulent loin meat, check with rib aficionados and local butchers to find who sells the best ribs. A meaty side of pork baby back ribs should weight at least 1.9 pounds.

Serving portion:

As an appetizer, 2 ribs per person. As an entrée, at least half a side per person.

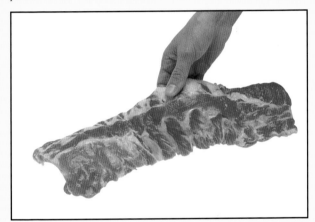

The King of Ribs

Country-Style Spareribs

These are meaty pieces from the rib end of the pork loin, and each piece contains a small bone. Boneless country-style spareribs are cut from the pork butt. These ribs are excellent smoked, grilled, roasted, or braised. Before cooking, always trim off all exterior fat.

Serving portion:

As an appetizer, 1 piece per person. As an entrée, half a pound per person if the ribs are boneless, or slightly more if they contain the bone.

BONELESS

Beef Back Ribs

It's fun to refer to these beef back ribs as "dinosaur bones," because it's impossible to display them or, for that matter, to eat them in a refined manner. From slabs cut from the loin and containing five or six bones, these ribs taste best smoked (our favorite way to cook them), grilled, or roasted. Because beef back ribs have so little meat, they are not as good as pork ribs when braised.

Serving portion:

As an appetizer, 2 ribs per person. As an entrée, 6 ribs per person.

Smoking Recommended!

Beef Short Ribs

Beef short ribs are cut from two areas of the steer. The most tender come from the bottom end of the rib cage, which curves under the belly (called the "plate"), and also from the chuck area. Short ribs are sold either cut between the ribs so that each piece has a single rib bone, or cut across the bones so that each piece contains two or more bones. For the meat to be tender, beef short ribs require hours of smoking or braising over very low heat. If you try to speed the cooking process by choosing grilling or roasting, the meat will be tough. Before cooking, always trim off all exterior fat.

Serving portion:

As an entrée, 1 pound of beef short ribs per person.

Smoke or braise over very low heat

Lamb Ribs

Many markets sell lamb "riblets." Each side weighs approximately 16 to 20 ounces. Because lamb ribs have so little meat, they are best smoked, grilled, or roasted, but not braised. Lamb ribs are very fatty and need to be carefully trimmed. This is a time-consuming step.

Serving portion:
As an appetizer, 3 ribs per person. As an entrée, 2 sides per person.

Rare and Exotic Ribs

We love the exotic and rare, such as buffalo ribs, elk ribs, venison ribs, and wild boar ribs. There's a primitive excitement about gnawing on giant buffalo ribs, the spicy sauce and juices dripping everywhere. We don't include recipes for exotic ribs, because these ribs rarely appear in markets. But if you are lucky enough to locate any of these, just follow the cooking principles outlined below, and then watch as eager crowds gather from throughout the neighborhood.

Preparation
and Cooking
Techniques

Fresh Versus Frozen

In most supermarkets, ribs are usually prefrozen and sold thawed. Whenever possible, buy fresh ribs (usually found in smaller specialty stores). Freezing destroys the cell structure. No matter how carefully the ribs are defrosted, they will never have the same juicy quality as fresh ribs. Also, compare local markets and buy the meatiest ribs.

Preliminary Boiling of Ribs

I am often asked by students whether I give the ribs a preliminary boiling/blanching in order to tenderize the ribs. Never. Never boil ribs. If you remove the membrane (see the following section) and cook the ribs over low heat, the ribs will be marvelously tender. Boiled ribs will never absorb the marinade, and the barbeque sauce will never form a beautiful layer across the surface during cooking.

Removing the Membrane

All ribs have a tough membrane that covers the underside (the nonmeaty side) of the ribs. This membrane is called the "fell." For all cooking techniques, remove the membrane or the ribs will always be tough. Most markets sell the ribs without removing the membrane. If you don't remember to ask the butcher to complete this task for you, here is a simple method for removing the membrane at home.

Place the ribs, meaty side down, on a flat surface. Using your fingernail, loosen a little of the membrane along the end of the last rib bone. Then, grasp the membrane firmly with a paper towel (so that the membrane doesn't slip from your grip). Holding the ribs down with the other hand, pull the membrane away. If it doesn't pull away in one piece, dislodge any remaining membrane, grip it with a paper towel, and pull the membrane away.

Marinating

For best taste, marinate the ribs in the refrigerator for 8 hours. The meat will be juicy and the marinade flavor will penetrate deeply into the rib meat. However, even if you marinate the ribs for just five minutes, the ribs will have a marvelous flavor if, during cooking, you baste them periodically with the marinade. Be sure not to brush any more marinade on the ribs during the last fifteen minutes of smoking, grilling, or oven roasting, so that any bacteria that the marinade absorbed from the raw meat will be killed. If you want to use the marinade as a sauce to accompany the ribs, reserve a portion of the marinade so that it never comes in contact with the raw meat or boil the meat marinade for one minute to kill any bacteria.

Basting

Basting ribs is essential when grilling, oven roasting, or smoking ribs. Basting helps keep the meat moist and creates a thicker coating on the ribs. Place the ribs on a baking sheet or roasting pan. For dry rubs, use your fingers to rub the mixture vigorously across both sides of the ribs. For marinades and slathers, coat both sides of the ribs using a basting brush, the underside of a spoon, or your hands. It's not necessary to rub the marinade into the meat; just coat the meat on all sides.

Dry Rubs, Marinades, Slathers...

Brown Paper Bag Technique

Here's a great optional technique that allows you to smoke, grill, or roast ribs before guests arrive and, if you are using spareribs or beef ribs, the meat will be even more tender. As soon as the ribs have been smoked, grilled, or roasted, transfer the ribs to a large supermarket paper bag, meaty side up. Fold the end of the bag closed and staple it shut. Be sure not to press the top of the bag into the surface of the ribs or the marinade will be rubbed off. Place the bag in a 140° oven for up to one hour. Then serve the ribs. The ribs "steam" in the bag, and the paper absorbs the fat.

Cutting Ribs

Never cut sides of ribs into individual ribs prior to smoking, grilling, or roasting. This causes the meat to dry out during cooking. If you have removed the side of ribs from the smoker, grill, or oven and plan to serve the ribs right away (and not keep them warm in a paper bag—see the previous section), wait five minutes before cutting them into individual ribs. When the ribs cool slightly they are easier to handle. Plus, internal juices that would have flooded onto the cutting board from the piping hot ribs are given time to be absorbed by the meat fiber, resulting in juicier meat. To carve, hold the meat with tongs while cutting between the bones. The best knives to use are a chef's knife, Chinese cleaver, or a Japanese slicing knife.

Grilling

Quick Directions

If using a gas barbecue, preheat it to medium (325°). If using charcoal or wood, prepare a fire. When the coals or wood are ash covered, push them to the outside of the grill. Place a pan of water in the bottom of the grill among the coals, and cover the coals with the cooking grate. Place a rib rack on the cooking grate and add the ribs. Alternatively, brush the cooking grate with a flavorless cooking oil, such as safflower oil, and then lay the ribs meaty side up in the center of the grill. Cover the grill. Regulate the heat so it remains at a medium temperature. Occasionally during cooking, baste the ribs with extra marinade. Grill the ribs until the meat begins to shrink from the ends of the rib bones. Approximate grilling times: pork baby back ribs and country-style spareribs, 75 minutes; spareribs and beef ribs, 90 minutes; lamb ribs, 40 minutes.

Grilled ribs are one of life's great taste sensations. With a little attention and low heat, ribs will stay moist and acquire an addictive, delicious barbecue flavor.

Equipment

A gas- or charcoal-fired grill large enough to hold a side of ribs is essential. You'll also need to have a tight-fitting lid to trap in all the smoky flavor.

Another essential piece of equipment is a "rib rack." By standing the ribs upright in the rack, you can cook many sides of ribs at the same time. Additionally, if the heat is a little too high, only the boned ends of the ribs become scorched.

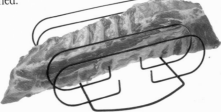

We also recommend spring-loaded tongs, heatproof mitts to protect your hands, an oven thermometer to place on the grill, and basting brushes made with natural hair (not nylon, which melts).

Preparing the Fire

If you don't have a gas barbecue, we recommend using
charcoal briquettes, which start easily, provide a steady heat,
and are available at every market. Lump hardwood charcoal
and hardwood such as oak provide superior flavor, but they
burn very hot, very fast, and are more likely to burn the food.
Use these only if you are a barbecue pro.

Choose one of the following ways to start the fire:

Lighter fluid. If you add a sprinkling of lighter
fluid, it will burn off as the coals heat and will not
give the food a "lighter fluid" taste. Mound the
charcoal into a peak and spray it with lighter fluid.
Place the lighter fluid at least ten feet away from the
grill, and then light the charcoal. Never reapply the
lighter fluid into coals that have already been
ignited. Fire can travel instantly up the stream of
lighter fluid and cause the container to explode.

Kindling. Crisscross dry sticks placed on top of
crumpled newspaper, add the charcoal in a mound,
and then light the newspaper.

Electric starters. Horseshoe-shaped electric
starters work very well. Place the horseshoe ring in
the center of the grill, add a mound of charcoal on

top, and then plug the cord into an electric outlet. In approximately ten minutes, all the coals lying on top of the starter will have lighted. At this point be sure to remove the electric starter or the fire will melt the plastic handle. If this occurs, the electric starter is no longer safe to use and must be discarded. Because the electric starter coil is extremely hot, when you remove it from the grill place it on an elevated heatproof shelf away from children, bare feet, and animals.

Metal chimney. Legions of backyard barbecue chefs love this device. Place a piece of crumpled newspaper in the bottom of the chimney, add charcoal, and then light the newspaper. In 20 minutes all the charcoal will have turned into glowing coals. With your hands in heatproof mitts, carefully lift out the chimney and the lighted charcoal will spill across the surface of the metal grate.

Nothing is more frustrating when grilling ribs than burning the ribs or having to finish cooking the ribs in the oven because the fire prematurely disappeared. It's always better to build a fire that is too large than to have the fire go out. To ensure that the ribs cook slowly, evenly, and without burning, use only the outer gas jets on gas barbecues. For charcoal fires, once the coals are ash-colored, push them to the edges of the barbecue. If the charcoal fire is still too hot, cover the grill and close the vents more. This robs the fire of oxygen, and the heat will quickly lower.

The heat is at the right temperature if, when you place your hand spread open about three inches above the fire, you're forced to remove your hand from the heat at the count of "1001, 1002, 1003."

Grilling the Ribs

Push the coals to the sides of the grill and place a pan of hot water in the center. The steam from the water makes the ribs more tender. Cover the coals with the cooking grate. Spray the rib rack with a nonstick spray and position the rack in the center of the cooking grate. Add the ribs (at room temperature) and cover the top. If you are not using a rib rack, turn the ribs over every ten minutes. Be sure to baste the ribs with reserved marinade (as described on page 20) 2 to 3 times on both sides during grilling. Regulate the temperature by raising or lowering the gas flames, or with charcoal fires, opening or closing the vents (remember that closing the vents lowers the heat). Place an oven thermometer on the grill or insert it into a vent on the lid so you can maintain the heat at medium (about 325°). The ribs are done when the meat begins to shrink from the ends of the rib bones.

Additional Techniques

To add flavor to the ribs, add hardwood chips, oak bark, or barrel staves. This is an especially useful technique for gas grills, because the gas flames and their vaporizing slats or lava rocks do not contribute the flavor that ribs acquire when cooked over briquettes, lump hardwood charcoal, and wood. Wood chips are available at supermarkets and hardware stores. Soak approximately 1 cup of chips in cold water for thirty minutes. Then drain them. Scatter the chips over the charcoal just before adding the ribs.

On gas grills, remove the cooking grill. Turn the gas jets on. Place the chips on a layer of aluminum foil and position this on the metal vaporizing slats or on the lava rocks at one corner of the grill. Reposition the cooking grill. Wait until the wood begins to smoke. Then place the ribs in the rib rack and cover the barbecue.

Smoking

Quick Smoking Directions

Preheat an electric smoker or build a small charcoal fire, bringing the temperature to 200° to 220°. When the coals are ash colored, push them to the outside of the smoker. Place a pan of hot water in the bottom of the smoker among the coals, and cover the coals with the cooking grate. Brush the cooking grate with flavorless cooking oil, such as safflower oil, and lay the ribs meaty side up in the center of the smoker or stand them upright in a rib rack. Cover the smoker. Regulate the heat so it remains at a medium temperature. Once an hour, brush the ribs with reserved marinade and add additional charcoal briquettes. Smoke the ribs until the meat begins to shrink away from the bones. Approximate smoking times: pork baby back ribs, spareribs, beef ribs, 3 hours; country-style spareribs, 3 to 4 hours; beef short ribs, 4 to 5 hours.

Slow smoking, what most Southerners call "barbecuing," means cooking ribs in a closed smoke-filled container where the heat is maintained at an even 200° to 220°. During the long time it takes to complete the cooking, ribs acquire a deep smoky flavor and become marvelously tender.

Equipment

There are hundreds of manufacturers of smokers, mostly located in the South. Inexpensive electric smokers are sold at most home discount centers nationwide, and smokers of all price ranges are sold by stores specializing in barbecue equipment. In case you are thinking about using a gas grill, don't! Gas grills can't maintain the low constant temperature required for slow smoking.

Other essential equipment are spring-loaded tongs, heatproof mitts, and a long-needled meat thermometer.

Preparing the Fire

For smoking, keep the heat low—200° to 220°. Light approximately 14 briquettes or lumps of hardwood charcoal to provide the heat for every 1 hour of smoking. Add 14 more lighted briquettes once an hour. Light the coals as described in the "Grilling" section, page 22. Once the coals are ash colored, push the coals around the sides of the grate, and place a pan of hot water in the center.

Insert the long-needled meat thermometer into one of the vents in the lid so you can easily monitor the temperature of the smoker.

While charcoal creates the heat, hardwood chips create the smoky flavor. You can use one wood or a blend of woods when smoking. Wood chip types to choose from include alder (light, delicate flavor); apple and cherry (sweet, fruity flavor); hickory (strong flavor); maple (sweet flavor); mesquite (pungent and will give food a bitter flavor with extended smoking); oak (assertive flavor and most versatile); and pecan (subtle, rich flavor).

Soak the chips as described in the "Grilling" section, page

22. Add just enough to maintain a smoky atmosphere. Because using large amounts of wood can give the food an overwhelming smoky, acrid flavor, it is better to use too little wood than too much. Be sure to shake excess water off wood chips before placing them on top of the hot charcoal.

Oven Roasting

Quick Roasting Directions

Preheat the oven to 350°. If your oven has a convection setting, set the oven on "convection" at 325°. Place the ribs on a wire rack, meaty side up. Place the rack on a foil-lined baking sheet on the middle oven rack. Place a small pan of hot water in the bottom of the oven, and roast the ribs until the meat begins to shrink from the ends of the bone. Brush the meaty side with reserved marinade one to two times during roasting. Do not turn the ribs over. Approximate roasting times: pork baby back ribs and country-style spareribs, 75 minutes; spareribs and beef ribs, 90 minutes; lamb ribs, 40 minutes.

Oven-roasted ribs, especially pork baby back ribs and spareribs, are delicious. Their wonderful smell drifting through the house creates the perfect welcoming note when guests arrive.

Equipment

Use a heavy baking sheet with shallow sides when oven-roasting ribs. Line the baking sheet with heavy-duty aluminum foil and then position a nonstick wire rack on top. Even with wire racks claiming to be "nonstick," spray the wire rack liberally on both sides with a nonstick vegetable oil cooking spray.

We also recommend spring-loaded tongs, heatproof mitts to protect your hands, and basting brushes made with natural hair (not nylon, which melts).

Roasting the Ribs

Preheat the oven to 350°. If your oven has a convection setting, set the oven on "convection" at 325°.

Place a small pan (such as a bread tin or small Pyrex dish) filled with 2 inches of hot tap water in the bottom of the oven, to keep the ribs from drying out as they roast.

Lay the ribs on the wire rack, meaty side up. Slide the pan holding the wire rack onto the center oven rack.

To prevent the ribs from steaming, cook only one baking pan of ribs per oven. Always roast the ribs meaty side up, and never turn the ribs over. Otherwise, the sauce glazing the meaty side of the ribs will be dislodged. Baste the meaty side of the ribs with reserved marinade (as described on page 20) two or three times during roasting.

Cook the ribs until the meat begins to shrink away from the ends of the bones, about 75 to 90 minutes.

Remove the ribs from the oven. Wait five minutes before cutting each rack into three pieces, in half, or into individual ribs.

Braising

Quick Braising Directions

Place a heavy stewpot over medium heat and preheat until it becomes hot. Add 2 to 4 tablespoons of cooking oil to the pot. When the oil gives off little wisps of smoke, add the ribs. Fry the ribs until they are lightly browned, about 5 minutes. Remove the ribs temporarily. Tip out and discard the oil. Return the ribs and add the previously prepared sauce. Bring to a low boil, cover the pot, and decrease the heat to low, so the sauce is at a simmer. Cook the ribs until the meat begins to shrink away from the bones, about 1 hour for pork ribs and 2 hours for beef short ribs. About every 15 minutes during cooking, stir the ribs. Once the meat shrinks away from the bones, temporarily remove the ribs. Using strips of paper towels, lift off all oil that is floating on the surface of the sauce. Return the ribs to the sauce and serve. Refrigerate the ribs if not serving them within 1 hour. Approximate braising times: pork baby back ribs, spareribs, and country-style spareribs, 1 hour; beef short ribs, 2 hours.

Braising is a great technique for ribs. After a few simple preparation steps, braising sets the cook free to pursue other activities, culinary or not. Because all rib meat is the equivalent of stew meat, long simmering breaks the connective tissue, renders fat, and transforms the texture of the meat from tough to succulent and tender.

Equipment

Choose a heavy 12- or 14-inch pan with 3-inch sides and a tight-fitting lid.

Preparation

Ask the butcher to cut across the bones, cutting the slab into 2-inch-wide strips. Remove the membrane from the underside of the ribs (see page 19). Then cut the ribs into lengths that will fit in the pan.

Cooking the Ribs

Preheat the pan until it becomes very hot, otherwise the ribs will stick when you try to brown them. Once the pan is hot, add 2 to 4 tablespoons of cooking oil. When the oil gives off little wisps of smoke, add the ribs.

You can brown the ribs in the oil (the oil splatters slightly) and then add the sauce used in the recipe, or, just before browning the ribs, lightly dust both sides of the ribs with white flour. Then brown the ribs and add the sauce. Or add the raw ribs, without browning, directly to the simmering sauce.

Keep the pan tightly covered. Regulate the heat so that the liquid is at a simmer with only a few bubbles rising to the surface, and never at a boil. If ribs are boiled, the meat becomes dry and flavorless.

The ribs are done when the meat is tender. For pork ribs, the meat has become tender when it shrinks away from the bones, usually after about 1 hour of gentle simmering. For beef short ribs, the meat shrinks from the bone long before the meat is tender. Simmer beef short ribs for about 2 hours, and always taste the meat to check whether it has become tender.

Before serving, remove all fat floating on the surface of the sauce. Otherwise the sauce tastes greasy. Once the ribs become tender, temporarily remove the ribs, and then, using strips of paper towel, skim the fat off the surface.

Lastly, if the sauce appears watery, it's easy to thicken it into a nice glaze. Mix one tablespoon of cornstarch with an equal amount of cold water. With the sauce at a simmer, stir in just enough of the cornstarch mixture to lightly thicken the sauce. Return the ribs to the pot. They can be served immediately or be left for up to 1 hour at room temperature and then gently reheated. If cooked further ahead than 1 hour, refrigerate the ribs. Braised ribs also taste delicious reheated the following day.

Combination Cooking Techniques

Ribs cooked using a combination of cooking techniques taste great. Try giving ribs a preliminary 2 hours of cooking in a smoker. Then, before they are fully cooked, finish the ribs on the grill or in a 325° oven, brushing them with the marinade. If grilling, baste them frequently for a complex smoky flavor and a beautiful glazed coating.

Or, smoke or grill the ribs, and then when they are still slightly undercooked, transfer them to a braising liquid.

Show-Stopping Asian Ribs

Best Chinese Baby Back Ribs

Serves 4

2 sides pork baby back ribs or your favorite type of ribs

CHINESE BARBECUE SAUCE

1 cup hoisin sauce

$^1/_2$ cup plum sauce

$^1/_3$ cup oyster sauce

$^1/_4$ cup wine vinegar

$^1/_4$ cup honey

2 tablespoons dark soy sauce

2 tablespoons dry sherry or Chinese rice wine

1 tablespoon dark sesame oil

1 tablespoon Asian chile sauce

$^1/_2$ teaspoon five-spice powder

1 tablespoon grated or finely minced orange zest

10 cloves garlic, finely minced

$^1/_4$ cup finely minced ginger

$^1/_4$ cup finely minced green onion, green and white parts

Remove the membrane from the underside of the ribs as shown on page 19. Then place the ribs in a rectangular dish or baking pan.

To make the sauce, combine all the sauce ingredients and stir well. Makes 3 cups.

Coat the ribs evenly on both sides with the marinade. Marinate the ribs, refrigerated, for at least 15 minutes. For more flavor, marinate for up to 8 hours.

To grill the ribs, if using a gas barbecue, preheat to medium (325°). If using charcoal or wood, prepare a fire. Grill according to the instructions on page 22. Occasionally during cooking, baste the ribs with extra sauce, stopping 15 minutes before removing the ribs from the grill.

To smoke the ribs, see page 27. To roast the ribs, see page 29.

To serve, cut each side of ribs in half, into 3 sections, or into individual ribs. Transfer to a heated serving platter or 4 heated dinner plates and serve at once.

Mahogany glaze is a classic Chinese sweet, sour, and mildly spicy marinade that takes only minutes to make. If you omit the green onions, the marinade can be made in large quantities and stored indefinitely in the refrigerator. Just add a little minced green onion to the portion of the marinade you plan to use that day. Although the ribs are excellent with just a brief marinating, when time allows, marinate the ribs all day. They'll have a more intense flavor and the marinade will turn an even darker mahogany color during cooking.

Mahogany Glazed Ribs

Serves 4

2 sides pork baby back ribs or your favorite ribs

GLAZE

1 cup hoisin sauce
$^3/_4$ cup plum sauce
$^1/_2$ cup thin soy sauce
$^1/_3$ cup cider vinegar
$^1/_4$ cup dry sherry or Chinese rice wine
$^1/_4$ cup honey
$^1/_2$ cup minced green onion, green and white parts
6 cloves garlic, finely minced

Remove the membrane from the underside of the ribs as shown on page 19. Then place the ribs in a rectangular dish or baking pan.

To make the glaze, combine all the glaze ingredients and stir well. Makes 3 $^1/_4$ cups.

Coat the ribs evenly on both sides with the glaze. Marinate the ribs, refrigerated, for at least 15 minutes. For more flavor, marinate for up to 8 hours.

To grill the ribs, if using a gas barbecue, preheat to medium (325°). If using charcoal or wood, prepare a fire. Grill according to the instructions on page 22. Occasionally during cooking, baste the ribs with extra glaze, stopping 15 minutes before removing the ribs from the grill.

To smoke the ribs, see page 27. To roast the ribs, see page 29.

To serve, cut each side of ribs in half, into 3 sections, or into individual ribs. Transfer to a heated serving platter or 4 heated dinner plates and serve at once.

"Curry" means a blend of seasonings and spices either ground into a paste or, if using only spices, toasted and powdered. Thai curries have no resemblance to Indian curries and this is particularly true for this red curry paste. The special ingredient here is lemongrass leaves, which have an intense lemon balm flavor. If you don't have lemongrass growing in your garden or being sold at a nearby Asian market, substitute 1 tablespoon of grated lemon zest.

Ribs with Thai Red Curry Sauce

Serves 4

2 pounds country-style spareribs (with bone) or your favorite ribs

4 cloves garlic, finely minced

2 tablespoons finely minced ginger

$^1/_2$ cup chopped roasted red bell peppers, bottled variety

1 cup seeded and chopped vine-ripened tomatoes

$^1/_4$ cup finely minced lemongrass leaves

Zest from 1 lime, minced

$^1/_3$ cup wine vinegar

$^1/_4$ cup Thai or Vietnamese fish sauce

$^1/_4$ cup honey

1 to 2 tablespoons Asian chile sauce

2 teaspoons ground coriander

2 teaspoons crushed red pepper flakes

Remove the membrane from the underside of the ribs as shown on page 19. Then place the ribs in a rectangular dish or baking pan.

To make the curry sauce, combine all the sauce ingredients in a food processor and purée. Makes 2 cups.

Coat the ribs evenly on both sides with the marinade. Marinate the ribs, refrigerated, for at least 15 minutes. For more flavor, marinate for up to 8 hours.

To grill the ribs, if using a gas barbecue, preheat to medium (325°). If using charcoal or wood, prepare a fire. Grill according to the instructions on page 22. Occasionally during cooking, baste the ribs with extra sauce, stopping 15 minutes before removing the ribs from the grill.

To smoke the ribs, see page 27. To roast the ribs, see page 29.

To serve, cut each side of ribs in half, into 3 sections, or into individual ribs. Transfer to a heated serving platter or 4 heated dinner plates and serve at once.

Thai Baby Back Ribs

Serves 4

2 sides pork baby back ribs or your favorite ribs

6 cloves garlic, minced

2 tablespoons finely minced ginger

8 serrano peppers or other small hot chiles, minced, including seeds

4 small green onions, green and white parts, minced

$1/4$ cup minced cilantro sprigs

1 tablespoon grated or minced lime zest

Juice from 3 limes

1 cup hoisin sauce

$1/2$ cup wine vinegar

$1/4$ cup Thai or Vietnamese fish sauce

$1/4$ cup honey

2 tablespoons dark soy sauce

2 tablespoons flavorless cooking oil

Remove the membrane from the underside of the ribs as described on page 19. Then place the ribs in a rectangular dish or baking pan.

To make the sauce, combine all the sauce ingredients and stir well. Makes 3 cups.

Coat the ribs evenly on both sides with half the sauce. Marinate the ribs, refrigerated, for at least 15 minutes. For more flavor, marinate for up to 8 hours. Reserve the remaining sauce to serve as a sauce for the ribs.

To grill the ribs, if using a gas barbecue, preheat to medium (325°). If using charcoal or wood, prepare a fire. Grill according to the instructions on page 22. Occasionally during cooking, baste the ribs with the marinade, stopping 15 minutes before removing the ribs from the grill.

To smoke the ribs, see page 27. To roast the ribs, see page 29.

To serve, cut each side of ribs in half, into 3 sections, or into individual ribs. Transfer to a heated serving platter or 4 heated dinner plates and serve at once accompanied by the reserved sauce.

Spicy Ribs in Lemongrass-Honey Glaze

Serves 4

2 sides spareribs or your favorite ribs

LEMONGRASS-HONEY GLAZE

$1/2$ cup finely minced lemongrass leaves, or 1 tablespoon minced lemon zest
Grated zest of 3 large limes, plus the juice
1 cup hoisin sauce
$1/4$ cup oyster sauce
$1/4$ cup dry sherry
$1/4$ cup honey
2 tablespoons Asian chile sauce
$1/4$ cup finely minced ginger
6 cloves garlic, finely minced
1 tablespoon chopped fresh cilantro sprigs
1 tablespoon chopped fresh basil
1 tablespoon chopped fresh mint

Remove the membrane from the underside of the ribs as shown on page 19. Then place the ribs in a rectangular dish or baking pan.

To make the glaze, combine all the glaze ingredients and stir well. Makes 3 cups.

Coat the ribs evenly on both sides with the glaze. Marinate the ribs, refrigerated, for at least 15 minutes. For more flavor, marinate for up to 8 hours.

To grill the ribs, if using a gas barbecue, preheat to medium (325°). If using charcoal or wood, prepare a fire. Grill according to the instructions on page 22. Occasionally during cooking, baste the ribs with extra glaze, stopping 15 minutes before removing the ribs from the grill.

To smoke the ribs, see page 27. To roast the ribs, see page 29.

To serve, cut each side of ribs in half, into 3 sections, or into individual ribs. Transfer to a heated serving platter or 4 heated dinner plates and serve at once.

Spareribs with Hoisin–Peanut Butter Rub

Serves 4

2 pounds country-style spareribs (bone in) or your favorite ribs

HOISIN–PEANUT BUTTER RUB

$^3/_4$ cup hoisin sauce
$^1/_2$ cup peanut butter, made from roasted, salted peanuts
$^1/_2$ cup plum sauce
$^1/_4$ cup oyster sauce
$^1/_4$ cup dry sherry or Chinese rice wine
$^1/_4$ cup dark soy sauce
2 tablespoons dark sesame oil
1 tablespoon Asian chile sauce
5 cloves garlic, finely minced
2 tablespoons finely minced ginger

Remove the membrane from the underside of the ribs as shown on page 19. Then place the ribs in a rectangular dish or baking pan.

To make the rub, combine all the rub ingredients and stir well. Makes 2 $^3/_4$ cups.

Coat the ribs evenly on both sides with the rub. Marinate the ribs, refrigerated, for at least 15 minutes. For more flavor, marinate for up to 8 hours.

To grill the ribs, if using a gas barbecue, preheat to medium (325°). If using charcoal or wood, prepare a fire. Grill according to the instructions on page 22. Occasionally during cooking, baste the ribs with extra rub, stopping 15 minutes before removing the ribs from the grill.

To smoke the ribs, see page 27. To roast the ribs, see page 29.

To serve, cut each side of ribs in half, into 3 sections, or into individual ribs. Transfer to a heated serving platter or 4 heated dinner plates and serve at once.

Szechuan Fire Ribs

Serves 4

2 sides of spareribs or your favorite ribs

SZECHUAN FIRE SAUCE

$^1/_4$ cup dry sherry or Chinese rice wine
$^1/_4$ cup hoisin sauce
$^1/_4$ cup thin soy sauce
$^1/_4$ cup oyster sauce
2 tablespoons wine vinegar
2 tablespoons dark sesame oil
2 tablespoons Asian chile sauce
2 teaspoons sugar
6 cloves garlic, finely minced
1 tablespoon finely minced ginger
2 green onions, green and white parts, minced
$^1/_4$ cup chopped cilantro sprigs

Remove the membrane from the underside of the ribs as shown on page 19. Then place the ribs in a rectangular dish or baking pan.

To make the sauce, combine all the sauce ingredients and stir well. Makes 1 $^3/_4$ cups.

Coat the ribs evenly on both sides with the sauce. Marinate the ribs, refrigerated, for at least 15 minutes. For more flavor, marinate for up to 8 hours.

To grill the ribs, if using a gas barbecue, preheat to medium (325°). If using charcoal or wood, prepare a fire. Grill according to the instructions on page 22. Occasionally during cooking, baste the ribs with extra sauce, stopping 15 minutes before removing the ribs from the grill.

To smoke the ribs, see page 27. To roast the ribs, see page 29.

To serve, cut each side of ribs in half, into 3 sections, or into individual ribs. Transfer to a heated serving platter or 4 heated dinner plates and serve at once.

Teriyaki Ribs

Serves 4

2 sides spareribs or your favorite ribs

TERIYAKI GLAZE

$^3/_4$ cup mirin (Japanese sweet sake)
$^3/_4$ cup sake
$^3/_4$ cup dark soy sauce
3 tablespoons sugar
1 tablespoon Asian chile sauce
$^1/_4$ cup finely minced ginger

Remove the membrane from the underside of the ribs as shown on page 19. Then place the ribs in a rectangular dish or baking pan.

To make the glaze, in a small saucepan, combine the mirin, sake, soy sauce, sugar, chile sauce, and ginger. Bring to a boil. Then set aside 1 cup to be used as the marinade. Boil the remaining sauce until only 1 cup remains. Set this aside to be used as the glaze.

Coat the ribs evenly on all sides with the marinade. Marinate the ribs, refrigerated, for at least 15 minutes. For more flavor, marinate for up to 8 hours.

To grill the ribs, if using a gas barbecue, preheat to medium (325°). If using charcoal or wood, prepare a fire. Grill according to the instructions on page 22. Occasionally during cooking, baste the ribs with the glaze, stopping 15 minutes before removing the ribs from the grill.

To smoke the ribs, see page 27. To roast the ribs, see page 29.

To serve, cut each side of ribs in half, into 3 sections, or into individual ribs. Transfer to a heated serving platter or 4 heated dinner plates and serve at once.

Asian pesto sauce is a combination of fresh herbs and Asian flavors liquefied in the blender, resulting in a deep green sauce. It's great brushed over ribs just before serving, or used as a side condiment to accompany any grilled fish or meat. Use the Asian Pesto sauce the day it is made, however, or the flavor will deteriorate. Moreover, never heat the sauce or the beautiful color and fresh sparkling flavors will be lost.

Ribs Rubbed with Asian Pesto

Serves 4

2 sides spareribs or your favorite ribs
¼ cup dark soy sauce
¼ cup freshly squeezed orange juice
1 tablespoon honey

ASIAN PESTO

1 ½ cups spinach leaves
1 cup mint leaves
10 basil leaves
¼ cup cilantro sprigs
1 small green onion, green and white parts
5 cloves garlic, finely minced
2 tablespoons finely minced ginger
1 teaspoon grated or finely minced orange zest
½ cup freshly squeezed orange juice
¼ cup distilled white vinegar
2 tablespoons dry sherry or Chinese rice wine
2 tablespoons thin soy sauce
2 tablespoons dark sesame oil
2 tablespoons hoisin sauce
1 tablespoon Asian chile sauce

Remove the membrane from the underside of the ribs as shown on page 19. Then place the ribs in a rectangular dish or baking pan.

Combine the soy sauce, orange juice, and honey. Rub this sauce over the ribs, coating them evenly. Marinate the ribs, refrigerated, for at least 15 minutes. For more flavor, marinate for up to 8 hours.

To make the pesto, place all ingredients in an electric blender. Blend into a liquid. Transfer the pesto to a bowl and refrigerate. Makes 2 cups.

To grill the ribs, if using a gas barbecue, preheat to medium (325°). If using charcoal or wood, prepare a fire. Grill according to the instructions on page 22. During the last 10 minutes of cooking, brush the ribs with the pesto.

To smoke the ribs, see page 27. During the last 10 minutes of cooking, brush the ribs with the pesto. To roast the ribs, see page 29.

To serve, brush the ribs with more pesto. Cut each side of ribs in half, into 3 sections, or into individual ribs. Transfer to a heated serving platter or 4 heated dinner plates and serve at once accompanied by any remaining pesto.

Pork Baby Back Ribs with Spicy Peanut Butter Slather

Serves 4

2 sides pork baby back ribs or your favorite ribs

$1/2$ cup chunky peanut butter, salted
$1/2$ cup dry sherry or Chinese rice wine
$1/4$ cup dark soy sauce
$1/4$ cup wine vinegar
$1/4$ cup honey
$1/4$ cup flavorless cooking oil
2 tablespoons dark sesame oil
2 tablespoons Asian chile sauce
Grated zest of 1 lime
6 cloves garlic, finely minced
$1/4$ cup finely minced ginger
$1/4$ cup minced green onion, green and white parts
$1/4$ cup minced cilantro sprigs

Remove the membrane from the underside of the ribs as shown on page 19. Then place the ribs in a rectangular dish or baking pan.

To make the marinade, combine all the marinade ingredients and stir well. Makes 2 $1/2$ cups.

Coat the ribs evenly on both sides with the marinade. Marinate the ribs, refrigerated, for at least 15 minutes. For more flavor, marinate for up to 8 hours.

To grill the ribs, if using a gas barbecue, preheat to medium (325°). If using charcoal or wood, prepare a fire. Grill according to the instructions on page 22. Occasionally during cooking, baste the ribs with extra marinade, stopping 15 minutes before removing the ribs from the grill.

To smoke the ribs, see page 27. To roast the ribs, see page 29.

To serve, cut each side of ribs in half, into 3 sections, or into individual ribs. Transfer to a heated serving platter or 4 heated dinner plates and serve at once.

Thai green curry sauce is a classic Thai seasoning rub—a kind of exotic pesto sauce—whose flavors linger on the palate long after the last bite. When making curry, it's important to use whole spices, such as coriander seeds, and to give them a preliminary toasting in an ungreased frying pan before powdering the spices in an electric spice grinder. The toasting intensifies their flavor. If you substitute store-bought ground spices, then do not toast.

Thai Green Curry Ribs

Serves 4

2 sides spareribs or your favorite ribs

GREEN CURRY RUB

4 whole cloves
12 black peppercorns
2 teaspoons coriander seeds
1 teaspoon caraway seeds
$1/2$ teaspoon cumin seeds
6 cloves garlic, peeled
1 medium shallot, peeled
3 whole serrano chiles, stemmed
$3/4$ cup fresh basil leaves
$3/4$ cup fresh cilantro sprigs
1 teaspoon salt
$1/2$ cup flavorless cooking oil

Remove the membrane from the underside of the ribs as shown on page 19. Then place the ribs in a rectangular dish or baking pan.

To make the rub, place the cloves, peppercorns, and coriander, caraway and cumin seeds in a small frying pan with no oil. Place the pan over medium heat and cook until the spices just begin to smoke, about 1 minute. Then, in an electric spice grinder, grind the spices into a powder. In a food processor, mince the garlic, shallot, and chiles. Remove the processor top. Add the basil, cilantro, and salt and mince very finely. Add the ground spices and mince again. Now with the machine running, slowly pour the cooking oil down the feed tube and mince until a paste is formed. Transfer to a small bowl. Makes approximately 1 cup.

Coat the ribs evenly on both sides with the curry rub. Marinate the ribs, refrigerated, for at least 15 minutes. For more flavor, marinate the ribs for up to 8 hours.

To grill the ribs, if using a gas barbecue, preheat to medium (325°). If using charcoal or wood, prepare a fire. Grill according to the instructions on page 22.

To smoke the ribs, see page 27. To roast the ribs, see page 29.

To serve, cut each side of ribs in half, into 3 sections, or into individual ribs. Transfer to a heated serving platter or 4 heated dinner plates and serve at once.

Tandoori Spareribs

Serves 4

2 sides of spareribs or your favorite ribs

TANDOORI MARINADE

$^1/_4$ cup plain yogurt

$^1/_3$ cup freshly squeezed lemon juice

4 dried red chiles, seeded

1 teaspoon black peppercorns

1 teaspoon cumin seeds

1 teaspoon coriander seeds

Seeds from 6 cardamom pods

$^1/_2$-inch stick cinnamon

1 teaspoon salt

1 teaspoon ground turmeric

$^1/_4$ teaspoon mace

6 cloves garlic

1-inch section of ginger root, thinly sliced

$^1/_4$ cup flavorless cooking oil

3 tablespoons honey

3 tablespoons minced green onion, green and white parts

2 tablespoons minced cilantro sprigs

1 teaspoon grated orange zest

Remove the membrane from the underside of the ribs as shown on page 19. Then place the ribs in a rectangular dish or baking pan.

To make the marinade, combine the yogurt and lemon juice in a bowl. In a small sauté pan, add the chiles, peppercorns, cumin, coriander, mustard, cardamom seeds, and cinnamon. Sauté over medium heat until the mustard seeds begin to pop, about 1 minute. Using a spice grinder, grind the spices into a powder. Transfer the powder to a bowl and add the salt, turmeric, nutmeg, and mace. In a food processor, mince the garlic and ginger. Add the ground spices and process briefly. With the processor on, slowly add the cooking oil and process into a paste. Add the honey and process briefly. Transfer the paste to the bowl containing the yogurt and lemon juice. Add the green onion, cilantro, and orange zest and stir well. Makes 1 cup.

Coat the ribs evenly on both sides with the marinade. Marinate the ribs, refrigerated, for 15 minutes. For more flavor, marinate for up to 8 hours.

To grill the ribs, if using a gas barbecue, preheat to medium (325°). If using charcoal or wood, prepare a fire. Grill according to the instructions on page 22. Occasionally during cooking, baste the ribs with extra marinade, stopping 15 minutes before removing the ribs from the grill.

To smoke the ribs, see page 27. To roast the ribs, see page 29.

To serve, cut each side of ribs in half, into 3 sections, or into individual ribs. Transfer to 4 heated dinner plates and serve at once.

New
Approaches
for American
Ribs

Ribs with All-Purpose Dry Rub and Sweet-and-Sour Mop

Serves 4

2 pounds country-style spareribs (with bone) or your favorite ribs

ALL-PURPOSE DRY RUB

1 tablespoon black peppercorns

1 tablespoon coriander seeds

1 teaspoon whole cloves

1 teaspoon mustard seeds

2 tablespoons sweet paprika

2 tablespoons chile powder

2 tablespoons light brown sugar

1 tablespoon dry mustard

1 teaspoon dried oregano

1 teaspoon dried thyme

1 teaspoon cayenne powder

SWEET-AND-SOUR MOP

1 cup Japanese rice vinegar, unseasoned

$^1/_4$ cup honey

$^1/_4$ cup olive oil

$^1/_4$ cup thin soy sauce

1 teaspoon crushed red pepper flakes

4 cloves garlic, finely minced

Remove the membrane from the underside of the ribs as shown on page 19. Then place the ribs in a rectangular dish or baking pan.

To make the rub, using an electric blender, grind the peppercorns, coriander, cloves, and mustard seeds to a powder. Transfer to a bowl, and add all the remaining rub ingredients. Stir well. Makes $^1/_2$ cup.

To make the mop, in a small bowl, combine the mop ingredients and stir well.

Coat the ribs evenly on both sides with half the rub. The remaining rub will last for 6 months sealed inside a jar and stored in your spice rack. Marinate the ribs, refrigerated, for at least 15 minutes. For more flavor, marinate for up to 24 hours.

To grill the ribs, if using a gas barbecue, preheat to medium (325°). If using charcoal or wood, prepare a fire. Grill according to the instructions on page 22. Occasionally during cooking, baste the ribs with the mop.

To smoke the ribs, see page 27. To roast the ribs, see page 29.

To serve, cut each side of ribs in half, into 3 sections, or into individual ribs. Transfer to a heated serving platter or 4 heated dinner plates and serve at once.

Spicy southern tomato glaze is a cascade of ingredients from hoisin to Heinz, soy to sesame, olive oil to onions. This glaze creates flavors both delectable and mysterious. The key technique is to brown the onions until they caramelize. Be patient, cooking the onions over low heat and stirring often. If you try to speed up the process by increasing the heat, the sugars in the onion will burn and the onion will not develop the necessary depth of flavor.

Sweet and Spicy Southern Tomato-Glazed Ribs

Serves 4

6 pounds beef ribs or your favorite ribs

SOUTHERN TOMATO GLAZE

$^1/_4$ cup olive oil

1 yellow onion, peeled and chopped

3 vine-ripened tomatoes

1 cup dry red wine

$^1/_2$ cup roasted red bell peppers, bottled variety

$^1/_2$ cup ketchup

$^1/_2$ cup hoisin sauce

$^1/_2$ cup Heinz 57 Sauce

$^1/_2$ cup cider vinegar

$^1/_4$ cup oyster sauce

$^1/_4$ cup honey

2 tablespoons dark soy sauce

1 tablespoon dark sesame oil

1 tablespoon chile powder

2 tablespoons chile sauce

8 cloves garlic, finely minced

$^1/_2$ cup minced ginger

$^1/_2$ cup chopped cilantro sprigs

2 tablespoons chopped oregano leaves

Remove the membrane from the underside of the ribs as shown on page 19. Then place the ribs in a rectangular dish or baking pan.

To make the marinade, place the olive oil and onion in a 12-inch sauté pan over medium heat. Sauté the onions until they brown, about 10 minutes. Add all the remaining ingredients and cook until the sauce becomes very thick. Allow the sauce to cool to room temperature. Then transfer to an electric blender and liquefy. Makes 3 cups.

Coat the ribs evenly on both sides with half the marinade. Marinate the ribs, refrigerated, for at least 15 minutes. For more flavor, marinate for up to 8 hours. Reserve the remaining marinade to serve as a sauce for the ribs.

To grill the ribs, if using a gas barbecue, preheat to medium (325°). If using charcoal or wood, prepare a fire. Grill according to the instructions on page 22. Occasionally during cooking, baste the ribs with extra marinade, stopping 15 minutes before removing the ribs from the grill.

To smoke the ribs, see page 27. To roast the ribs, see page 29.

To serve, cut each side of ribs in half, into 3 sections, or into individual ribs. Transfer to a heated serving platter or 4 heated dinner plates and serve at once accompanied by the reserved sauce.

Try a Louisiana-style sauce with charred tomatoes and onions simmered in a spicy red wine sauce. The key technique is to grill sliced tomatoes and onions over a gas or charcoal fire before simmering them with the rest of the ingredients. For even more flavor, sprinkle 1/2 cup of hardwood chips onto the coals just before adding the onions and tomatoes. Cover the grill tightly so that the onions and tomatoes acquire a smoky taste.

Ribs Louisiana Style

Serves 4

2 sides spareribs or your favorite ribs

2 vine-ripened tomatoes
2 small yellow onions
$^1/_4$ cup chopped roasted red bell peppers, bottled variety
1 cup dry red wine
$^1/_2$ cup ketchup
$^1/_2$ cup cider vinegar
2 tablespoons honey
2 tablespoons Worcestershire sauce
2 tablespoons extra virgin olive oil
1 tablespoon Tabasco sauce
1 tablespoon chile sauce
4 cloves garlic, finely minced
2 tablespoons minced oregano leaves
2 tablespoons chopped fresh thyme leaves
1 teaspoon minced orange zest

Remove the membrane from the underside of the ribs as shown on page 19. Then place the ribs in a rectangular dish or baking pan.

To make the marinade, cut each tomato into 3 slices. Peel and cut each onion into 3 slices. Heat a gas grill or build a fire. Soak $^1/_2$ cup of wood chips according to the directions on page 26. When the coals are ash colored, scatter the wood chips over the coals. Brush the cooking grate with oil. Place the tomatoes and onions on the grill. Cover the grill and smoke the tomatoes and onions 15 to 20 minutes, turning them once, until they are golden. Discard the tomato skins. Transfer the tomatoes and onions to a food processor and chop coarsely. Transfer the mixture to a saucepan and add the remaining ingredients. Bring to a boil. Boil until only 3 cups remain. Transfer the marinade to a small bowl and allow it cool to room temperature.

Coat the ribs evenly on both sides with half the marinade. Marinate the ribs, refrigerated, for at least 15 minutes. For more flavor, marinate for up to 8 hours. Reserve the remaining marinade to serve as a sauce for the ribs.

To grill the ribs, if using a gas barbecue, preheat to medium (325°). If using charcoal or wood, prepare a fire. Grill according to the instructions on page 22. Occasionally during cooking, baste the ribs with extra marinade, stopping 15 minutes before removing the ribs from the grill.

To smoke the ribs, see page 27. To roast the ribs, see page 29.

To serve, cut each side of ribs in half, into 3 sections, or into individual ribs. Transfer to a heated serving platter or 4 heated dinner plates and serve at once accompanied by the reserved sauce.

Spareribs with Mustard, Soy, and Juniper Berry Rub

Serves 4

2 sides spareribs or your favorite ribs

$1/4$ cup Dijon mustard

3 tablespoons thin soy sauce

3 tablespoons wine vinegar

3 tablespoons honey

2 teaspoons juniper berries, crushed

$1/2$ teaspoon freshly ground black pepper

6 cloves garlic, finely minced

2 fresh serrano chiles

Remove the membrane from the underside of the ribs as shown on page 19. Then place the ribs in a rectangular dish or baking pan.

To make the rub, combine all the rub ingredients and stir well. Makes 1 cup.

Coat the ribs evenly on both sides with the rub. Marinate the ribs, refrigerated, for at least 15 minutes. For more flavor, marinate for up to 8 hours.

To grill the ribs, if using a gas barbecue, preheat to medium (325°). If using charcoal or wood, prepare a fire. Grill according to the instructions on page 22. Occasionally during cooking, baste the ribs with extra rub, stopping 15 minutes before removing the ribs from the grill.

To smoke the ribs, see page 27. To roast the ribs, see page 29.

To serve, cut each side of ribs in half, into 3 sections, or into individual ribs. Transfer to a heated serving platter or 4 heated dinner plates and serve at once.

Spicy Pirate Ribs
with Lemon Mop

Serves 4

2 pounds country-style spareribs (with bone) or your favorite ribs

SPICY PIRATE RUB

4 cloves garlic, finely minced

18 allspice berries

1-inch piece cinnamon

1 teaspoon black peppercorns

1 teaspoon coriander seeds

1/2 teaspoon whole cloves

1/4 cup dark brown sugar

3 tablespoons chile powder

1 tablespoon dried thyme

2 teaspoons powdered mustard

1 1/2 teaspoons salt

1 teaspoon freshly ground nutmeg

SPICY LEMON MOP

1 tablespoon finely minced lemon zest

1/2 cup freshly squeezed lemon juice

1/4 cup light brown sugar

1/4 cup chile sauce

Remove the membrane from the underside of the ribs as shown on page 19. Then place the ribs in a rectangular dish or baking pan.

Rub the garlic over both sides of the ribs.

Place the allspice, cinnamon, peppercorns, coriander, and cloves in a small ungreased sauté pan over medium heat and toast until the spices just begin to smoke. Then grind the spices finely in an electric spice grinder. In a small bowl, combine the ground spices with the rest of the rub ingredients and stir to evenly combine.

Using your fingers or a spoon, rub the rub evenly on both sides of the ribs. Marinate the ribs, refrigerated, for at least 15 minutes. For more flavor, marinate for up to 8 hours. In a small bowl, combine the ingredients for the Spicy Lemon Mop, and refrigerate.

To grill the ribs, if using a gas barbecue, preheat to medium (325°). If using charcoal or wood, prepare a fire. Grill according to the instructions on page 22. Occasionally during grilling, baste the ribs with the mop, stopping 15 minutes before removing the ribs from the grill.

To smoke the ribs, see page 27. To roast the ribs, see page 29.

To serve, cut each side of ribs in half, into 3 sections, or into individual ribs. Transfer to a heated serving platter or 4 heated dinner plates and serve at once.

Pork Baby Back Ribs with Spicy Asian Chipotle Chile Sauce

Serves 4

2 sides pork baby back ribs or your favorite type of ribs

MARINADE

$^1/_4$ cup chipotle chiles in adobo sauce, minced

1 cup hoisin sauce

1 cup plum sauce

$^1/_3$ cup oyster sauce

$^1/_4$ cup dark soy sauce

$^1/_4$ cup distilled white vinegar

3 tablespoons flavorless cooking oil

3 tablespoons honey

6 cloves garlic, finely minced

2 tablespoons finely minced ginger

1 teaspoon minced orange zest

Remove the membrane from the underside of the ribs as shown on page 19. Then place the ribs in a rectangular dish or baking pan.

To make the marinade, combine all the marinade ingredients in a bowl. Makes 3 $^1/_2$ cups.

Coat the ribs evenly on both sides with the marinade. Marinate the ribs, refrigerated, for at least 15 minutes. For more flavor, marinate for up to 8 hours.

To grill the ribs, if using a gas barbecue, preheat to medium (325°). If using charcoal or wood, prepare a fire. Grill according to the instructions on page 22. Occasionally during cooking, baste the ribs with extra marinade, stopping the basting process 15 minutes before the ribs are removed from the grill.

To smoke the ribs, see page 27. To roast the ribs, see page 29.

To serve, cut each side of ribs in half, into 3 sections, or into individual ribs. Transfer to a heated serving platter or 4 heated dinner plates and serve at once.

Carolina Barbecued Ribs

Serves 4

2 sides pork baby back ribs or your favorite ribs
$1/4$ cup chile powder
1 tablespoon ground black pepper
1 tablespoon brown sugar
2 teaspoons crushed red pepper flakes
2 teaspoons garlic powder
1 teaspoon dried thyme

CAROLINA MOUNTAIN BARBECUE SAUCE

1 medium yellow onion
2 teaspoons olive oil
4 cloves garlic, finely minced
1 cup brown sugar
2 cups ketchup
$3/4$ cup apple cider vinegar
$1/2$ cup thin soy sauce
2 tablespoons Worcestershire sauce
1 teaspoon crushed red pepper flakes
1 teaspoon dry mustard
1 tablespoon finely minced ginger

Remove the membrane from the underside of the ribs as shown on page 19. Then place the ribs in a rectangular dish or baking pan.

In a small bowl, combine the chile powder, pepper, sugar, crushed red pepper, garlic powder, and thyme and mix well. Using your fingers, rub the mixture over both sides of the ribs. Marinate the ribs, refrigerated, for at least 15 minutes. For more flavor, marinate for up to 24 hours.

To make the barbecue sauce, slice the onion into $1/4$-inch slices. Place the slices in a stovetop smoker and smoke them over hickory sawdust for 10 minutes. Alternatively, grill or broil the onion slices until they are dark golden. Transfer the onion slices to a saucepan and add the remaining barbecue sauce ingredients. Bring to a simmer, reduce heat to low, cover, and simmer for 30 minutes. Pour the sauce through a medium-meshed strainer, scraping the sieve with a metal spoon to force all the pulp through the sieve. Makes 3 cups. Refrigerate the sauce.

To grill the ribs, if using a gas barbecue, preheat to medium (325°). If using charcoal or wood, prepare a fire. Grill according to the instructions on page 22. Occasionally during cooking, baste the ribs with barbecue sauce, stopping 15 minutes before removing the ribs from the grill.

To smoke the ribs, see page 27. To roast the ribs, see page 29.

To serve, cut each side of ribs in half, into 3 sections, or into individual ribs. Transfer to a heated serving platter or 4 heated dinner plates and serve at once, accompanied by any extra sauce.

Many Mexican chiles have become staples in our pantry. Fruity ancho chiles and smoky, fiery hot chipotle chiles are balanced by honey, wine vinegar, and cilantro. Look for ancho and chipotle chiles in the Mexican section of your supermarket or order them from a gourmet products catalog.

Spareribs with Cowboy Rub

Serves 4

2 sides of spareribs or your favorite ribs

COWBOY RUB

2 1/2 ounces ancho chiles, about 4
1/4 cup chipotle chiles in adobo sauce
1/4 cup wine vinegar
1/4 cup thin soy sauce
1/4 cup honey
3 tablespoons olive oil
1 small shallot, minced
8 cloves garlic, finely minced
1/4 cup chopped cilantro sprigs

Remove the membrane from the underside of the ribs as shown on page 19. Then place the ribs in a rectangular dish or baking pan.

To make the rub, place the ancho chiles in a bowl and cover with boiling water. Place a small saucer on the chiles to submerge them. After 30 minutes, stem the chiles and wash away the seeds. Place the ancho chiles and the chipotle chiles in a food processor. Blend until the chiles are thoroughly puréed. Add all the remaining rub ingredients. Blend again to evenly mix. Makes 1 1/2 cups.

Coat the ribs evenly on both sides with the marinade. Marinate the ribs, refrigerated, for at least 15 minutes. For more flavor, marinate the ribs for up to 8 hours.

To grill the ribs, if using a gas barbecue, preheat to medium (325°). If using charcoal or wood, prepare a fire. Grill according to the instructions on page 22. Occasionally during cooking, baste the ribs with extra rub, stopping 15 minutes before removing the ribs from the grill.

To smoke the ribs, see page 27. To roast the ribs, see page 29.

To serve, cut each side of ribs in half, into 3 sections, or into individual ribs. Transfer to a heated serving platter or 4 heated dinner plates and serve at once.

NEW APPROACHES FOR AMERICAN RIBS

Cajun Pepper Mustard-Crusted Ribs

Serves 4

2 sides spareribs or your favorite ribs

CAJUN PEPPER MUSTARD CRUST

$^1/_2$ tablespoon black peppercorns

$^1/_2$ tablespoon red peppercorns

$^1/_2$ tablespoon white peppercorns

$^1/_2$ tablespoon green peppercorns

1 teaspoon mustard seeds

1 teaspoon coriander seeds

$^1/_2$ cup Cajun mustard

$^1/_4$ cup olive oil

$^1/_4$ cup freshly squeezed lemon juice

2 tablespoons Worcestershire sauce

1 tablespoon chile sauce

2 tablespoons minced fresh basil leaves

1 tablespoon minced fresh thyme and leaves

4 cloves garlic, finely minced

Remove the membrane from the underside of the ribs as shown on page 19. Then place the ribs in a rectangular dish or baking pan.

To make the crust, using an electric spice grinder, very coarsely grind the peppercorns. Then set them aside in a bowl. Finely grind the mustard and coriander into a powder. Transfer to the bowl holding the ground pepper. Add all the remaining ingredients, and stir well. Makes 1 cup.

Coat the ribs evenly on both sides with the crust. Marinate the ribs, refrigerated, for at least 15 minutes. For more flavor, marinate for up to 8 hours.

To grill the ribs, if using a gas barbecue, preheat to medium (325°). If using charcoal or wood, prepare a fire. Grill according to the instructions on page 22. Occasionally during cooking, baste the ribs with extra glaze, stopping 15 minutes before removing the ribs from the grill.

To smoke the ribs, see page 27. To roast the ribs, see page 29.

To serve, cut each side of ribs in half, into 3 sections, or into individual ribs. Transfer to a heated serving platter or 4 heated dinner plates and serve at once.

Amazing Ribs with Amazing Glaze

Serves 4

6 pounds beef ribs or your favorite ribs

AMAZING GLAZE

1 tablespoon olive oil

$^1/_2$ cup chopped yellow onion

6 cloves garlic, finely minced

2 tablespoons minced fresh thyme leaves

2 cups dry red wine

1 $^1/_2$ cups ketchup

$^1/_4$ cup Heinz 57 Sauce

3 tablespoons brown sugar

2 tablespoons dark sesame oil

2 tablespoons chile powder

1 tablespoon molasses

1 tablespoon dried oregano

1 tablespoon paprika

$^1/_2$ tablespoon dried sage

$^1/_2$ tablespoon Tabasco sauce

Remove the membrane from the underside of the ribs as shown on page 19. Then place the ribs in a rectangular dish or baking pan.

To make the glaze, add the olive oil and onion to a 2 $^1/_2$-quart saucepan. Place the saucepan over medium-low heat and cook until the onion becomes translucent, about 10 minutes. Add the garlic and sauté for 30 seconds. Add all the remaining ingredients. Bring to a low boil, cover, and decrease the heat to a simmer. Allow the glaze to simmer for 20 minutes. Then remove the lid, turn the heat to high, and boil the glaze until only 3 cups remain. Transfer the glaze to a bowl and allow it to cool to room temperature.

Coat the ribs evenly on both sides with half the glaze. Marinate the ribs, refrigerated, for at least 15 minutes. For more flavor, marinate for up to 8 hours. Reserve the remaining glaze to serve as a sauce for the ribs.

To grill the ribs, if using a gas barbecue, preheat to medium (325°). If using charcoal or wood, prepare a fire. Grill according to the instructions on page 22. Occasionally during cooking, baste the ribs with the marinade, stopping 15 minutes before removing the ribs from the grill.

To smoke the ribs, see page 27. To roast the ribs, see page 29.

To serve, cut each side of ribs in half, into 3 sections, or into individual ribs. Transfer to a heated serving platter or 4 heated dinner plates and serve at once, accompanied by the reserved sauce.

Ribs Marinated with Molasses-Chile Barbecue Sauce

Serves 4

6 pounds beef ribs or your favorite ribs

MOLASSES-CHILE BARBECUE SAUCE

2 tablespoons extra virgin olive oil

$1/2$ cup peeled and chopped horseradish root

1 small yellow onion, peeled and chopped

6 cloves garlic, chopped

3 serrano chiles, chopped, including seeds

2 tablespoons minced ginger

2 vine-ripened tomatoes, seeded and chopped

$1/4$ cup chopped roasted red bell peppers, bottled variety

$1/2$ cup dry red wine

$1/2$ cup white distilled vinegar

$1/4$ cup molasses

$1/4$ cup dark corn syrup

2 tablespoons dark soy sauce

1 tablespoon Tabasco sauce

1 ounce anchovy fillets, packed in oil

2 teaspoons dried thyme

Remove the membrane from the underside of the ribs as shown on page 19. Then place the ribs in a rectangular dish or baking pan.

To make the sauce, place the olive oil, horseradish, and onion in a 12-inch sauté pan placed over medium heat. Sauté the onion for about 10 minutes, stirring occasionally, until the onion browns. Then add the garlic, chiles, ginger, tomatoes, and peppers. Sauté for 5 minutes. Add the remaining sauce ingredients and stir well. Simmer over lowest heat, uncovered, for 30 minutes. Allow the sauce to cool to room temperature. Transfer to a blender, and liquefy. Makes 2 cups.

Coat the ribs evenly on both sides with the sauce. Marinate the ribs, refrigerated, for at least 15 minutes. For more flavor, marinate for up to 8 hours.

To grill the ribs, if using a gas barbecue, preheat to medium (325°). If using charcoal or wood, prepare a fire. Grill according to the instructions on page 22. Occasionally during cooking, baste the ribs, stopping 15 minutes before removing the ribs from the grill.

To smoke the ribs, see page 27. To roast the ribs, see page 29.

To serve, cut each side of ribs in half, into 3 sections, or into individual ribs. Transfer to a heated serving platter or 4 heated dinner plates and serve at once.

Crushed Peppercorn and Orange Glazed Ribs

Serves 4

6 pounds beef ribs or your favorite ribs

CRUSHED PEPPERCORN AND ORANGE GLAZE

$^1/_2$ tablespoon red peppercorns

$^1/_2$ tablespoon black peppercorns

$^1/_2$ tablespoon white peppercorns

$^1/_2$ tablespoon green peppercorns

1 tablespoon minced orange zest

$^1/_2$ cup freshly squeezed orange juice

$^1/_2$ cup hoisin sauce

$^1/_4$ cup wine vinegar

5 cloves garlic, finely minced

$^1/_4$ cup minced green onions, green and white parts

$^1/_4$ cup minced cilantro sprigs

Remove the membrane from the underside of the ribs as shown on page 19. Then place the ribs in a rectangular dish or baking pan.

To make the glaze, place the peppercorns in a spice grinder and grind them to a powder. Rub the ground pepper across the surface of the meat. In a bowl, combine all the remaining glaze ingredients and stir well. Makes 1 $^1/_3$ cups.

Coat the ribs evenly on both sides with the glaze. Marinate the ribs, refrigerated, for at least 15 minutes. For more flavor, marinate for up to 8 hours.

To grill the ribs, if using a gas barbecue, preheat to medium (325°). If using charcoal or wood, prepare a fire. Grill according to the instructions on page 22. Occasionally during cooking, baste the ribs with extra glaze, stopping 15 minutes before removing the ribs from the grill.

To smoke the ribs, see page 27. To roast the ribs, see page 29.

To serve, cut each side of ribs in half, into 3 sections, or into individual ribs. Transfer to a heated serving platter or 4 heated dinner plates and serve at once.

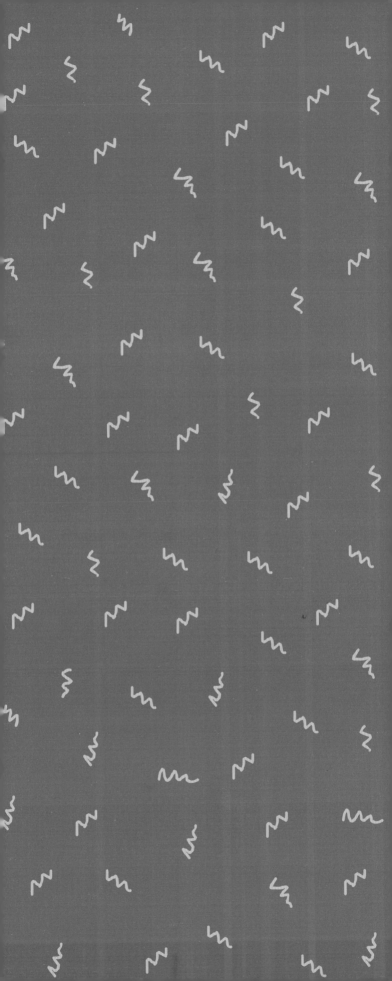

Mexican and Southwestern Masterpieces

Ancho Chile–Glazed Ribs

Serves 4

2 sides spareribs or your favorite ribs

ANCHO RUB

$1/4$ pound ancho chiles, about 6 chiles

1 cup freshly squeezed orange juice

3 tablespoons red currant jelly or raspberry jam

2 tablespoons honey

1 tablespoon red wine vinegar

$1/2$ teaspoon salt

$1/4$ teaspoon ground cloves

$1/4$ teaspoon ground allspice

5 cloves garlic, peeled

1 small shallot, peeled

Remove the membrane from the underside of the ribs as shown on page 19. Then place the ribs in a rectangular dish or baking pan.

To make the rub, place the ancho chiles in a bowl and cover them with boiling water. After 30 minutes, stem the chiles and wash away the seeds. Place the ancho chiles in a food processor fitted with a metal blade and mince finely. Add all the remaining rub ingredients and blend until very smooth. Makes 2 cups.

Coat the ribs evenly on both sides with half the rub. Marinate the ribs, refrigerated, for at least 15 minutes. For more flavor, marinate for up to 8 hours.

To grill the ribs, if using a gas barbecue, preheat to medium (325°). If using charcoal or wood, prepare a fire. Grill according to the instructions on page 22. Occasionally during cooking, baste the ribs, stopping 15 minutes before removing the ribs from the grill.

To smoke the ribs, see page 27. To roast the ribs, see page 29.

To serve, cut each side of ribs in half, into 3 sections, or into individual ribs. Transfer to a heated serving platter or 4 heated dinner plates and serve at once.

Ribs with Oaxacan Mole Sauce

Serves 4

2 pounds country-style spareribs (with bone) or your favorite ribs
Sweet Nutmeg Rub (see page 120)

MOLE SAUCE

2 tablespoons almonds
1 tablespoon white sesame seeds
2 ancho chiles
2 tablespoons dark raisins
3 cups boiling water
1 $^1/_2$ tablespoons olive oil
2 medium vine-ripened tomatoes, seeded and chopped
$^1/_2$ medium yellow onion, peeled and chopped
4 cloves garlic, minced
2 tablespoons oyster sauce
1 tablespoon chile sauce or spicy chile powder
$^1/_2$ teaspoon ground cinnamon
$^1/_2$ teaspoon salt
$^1/_2$ teaspoon allspice
$^1/_2$ teaspoon dried oregano
$^1/_2$ teaspoon freshly ground black pepper
$^1/_4$ teaspoon dried thyme
$^1/_8$ teaspoon ground cloves
1 ounce Ibarra Mexican chocolate or bittersweet chocolate, chopped

Remove the membrane from the underside of the ribs as shown on page 19. Then place the ribs in a rectangular dish or baking pan.

Rub the nutmeg rub on both sides of the ribs. Marinate the ribs, refrigerated, for at least 15 minutes. For more flavor, marinate for up to 8 hours.

To make the mole, toast the almonds in a 325° oven for 12 minutes, or until golden. In an ungreased skillet over high heat, brown the sesame seeds until golden. Place the ancho chiles and raisins in a bowl, and cover with the boiling water. After 30 minutes, drain the chiles and raisins, reserving the chile water. Stem and seed the chiles. In a food processor fitted with a metal blade, finely grind the almonds and sesame seeds. Add the ancho chiles and $^1/_2$ cup of the ancho chile water. Liquefy. In a 12-inch sauté pan over medium heat, add the ancho chile mixture, 1 cup of the ancho chile water, and all the other sauce ingredients except the chocolate. Bring to a boil. Then decrease the heat and allow the sauce to simmer until it becomes very thick, about 30 minutes. Stir in the chocolate. Simmer 5 more minutes. Then transfer to a blender and finely chop. Allow the sauce to cool to room temperature. Makes 2 cups.

To grill the ribs, if using a gas barbecue, preheat to medium (325°). If using charcoal or wood, prepare a fire. Grill according to the instructions on page 22. Occasionally during cooking, baste the ribs with the mole.

To smoke the ribs, see page 27. To roast the ribs, see page 29.

To serve, warm the remaining mole in a saucepan. Cut each side of ribs in half, into 3 sections, or into individual ribs. Transfer to a heated serving platter or 4 heated dinner plates and serve at once accompanied by the mole.

Chipotle chiles are smoked fresh jalapeño peppers, dried and then submerged in a very rich adobo sauce. These are extraordinarily spicy. To tame this sauce, reduce the amount of chipotle chiles to 1 tablespoon and add ½ cup of ketchup or a bottled mild tomato chile sauce.

Sweet-and-Sour Fiery Ribs

Serves 4

6 pounds beef ribs or your favorite ribs

FIERY SAUCE

$^{1}/_{2}$ cup honey
$^{1}/_{2}$ cup water
$^{1}/_{2}$ cup distilled white vinegar
$^{1}/_{2}$ cup chipotle chiles in adobo sauce
$^{1}/_{2}$ cup tomato paste
1 teaspoon ground cinnamon
1 cup chopped cilantro sprigs
6 cloves garlic, finely minced

Remove the membrane from the underside of the ribs as shown on page 19. Then place the ribs in a rectangular dish or baking pan.

To make the sauce, combine all the sauce ingredients in a food processor fitted with a metal blade and purée. Makes 2 $^{1}/_{2}$ cups.

Coat the ribs evenly on both sides with half the sauce. Marinate the ribs, refrigerated, for at least 15 minutes. For more flavor, marinate for up to 8 hours. Reserve the remaining sauce to serve as a sauce for the ribs.

To grill the ribs, if using a gas barbecue, preheat to medium (325°). If using charcoal or wood, prepare a fire. Grill according to the instructions on page 22. Occasionally during cooking, baste the ribs with the marinade, stopping 15 minutes before removing the ribs from the grill.

To smoke the ribs, see page 27. To roast the ribs, see page 29.

To serve, cut each side of ribs in half, into 3 sections, or into individual ribs. Transfer to a heated serving platter or 4 heated dinner plates and serve at once accompanied by the reserved sauce.

In a chipotle chile marinade, garlic, honey, molasses, vinegar, and cumin become the players performing on the chipotle chile stage. To create a mellow garlic flavor, garlic cloves are first rubbed with olive oil, then sealed in foil and roasted in the oven. It's a simple step to squeeze the garlic flesh away from the skin and blend it with the rest of the ingredients in a food processor.

Ribs Rubbed with Secret Chipotle-Honey Barbecue Sauce

Serves 4

2 sides of spareribs or your favorite ribs

CHIPOTLE-HONEY BARBECUE SAUCE

10 cloves garlic, with skin
1 tablespoon olive oil
2 medium vine-ripened tomatoes
$^1/_4$ cup minced fresh oregano
$^1/_4$ cup chipotle chiles in adobo sauce
$^1/_4$ cup cider vinegar
2 tablespoons honey
2 tablespoons molasses
2 tablespoons dark sesame oil
1 tablespoon cumin
1 teaspoon salt

Remove the membrane from the underside of the ribs as shown on page 19. Then place the ribs in a rectangular dish or baking pan.

To make the barbecue sauce, preheat the oven to 450°. Rub the garlic cloves with oil. Seal the cloves airtight but loosely in aluminum foil. Place in the oven and roast for 30 minutes. Then squeeze the garlic from its peel. Cut the tomatoes in half and char the halves on both sides on an outdoor grill or under the broiler until nearly black. Place all the barbecue sauce ingredients in a food processor. Purée until smooth. Makes 2 cups.

Coat the ribs evenly on both sides with half the sauce. Marinate the ribs, refrigerated, for at least 15 minutes. For more flavor, marinate for up to 8 hours. Reserve the remaining sauce to serve as a sauce for the ribs.

To grill the ribs, if using a gas barbecue, preheat to medium (325°). If using charcoal or wood, prepare a fire. Grill according to the instructions on page 22. Occasionally during cooking, baste the ribs with extra marinade, stopping 15 minutes before removing the ribs from the grill.

To smoke the ribs, see page 27. To roast the ribs, see page 29.

To serve, cut each side of ribs in half, into 3 sections, or into individual ribs. Transfer to a heated serving platter or 4 heated dinner plates and serve at once accompanied by the sauce.

1 teaspoon

Dried ancho and fresh serrano chiles are the flavor building blocks that provide a "Southwest" taste to a barbecue sauce. If you don't have ancho chiles, which have a wonderful fruity flavor, omit the anchos and replace the honey with red currant jelly.

Southwest Chile Barbecued Ribs

Serves 4

2 sides pork baby back ribs or your favorite ribs

2 ancho chiles
4 large vine-ripened tomatoes, seeded and chopped
1 cup chopped mango flesh, from about 2 mangoes
$1/4$ cup chopped roasted red bell peppers, bottled variety
5 cloves garlic, finely minced
$1/4$ cup minced ginger
4 serrano chiles, finely minced, including the seeds
1 tablespoon grated and minced orange skin
1 cup freshly squeezed orange juice
$1/2$ cup wine vinegar
$1/4$ cup thin soy sauce
$1/4$ cup honey
2 teaspoons curry powder
$1/2$ teaspoon ground cloves

Remove the membrane from the underside of the ribs as shown on page 19. Then place the ribs in a rectangular dish or baking pan.

To make the sauce, place the ancho chiles in a bowl and cover with boiling water. Place a small saucer on the chiles to submerge them. After 30 minutes, stem the chiles and wash away the seeds. Save $1/2$ cup of the ancho water. Place the ancho chiles in a food processor fitted with a metal blade, add $1/2$ cup ancho water, and purée. Add all the remaining sauce ingredients and purée. Transfer to a 3-quart saucepan. Bring the sauce to a boil, and allow it to boil until the sauce reduces to 3 cups, about 20 minutes. Then allow the sauce to cool to room temperature.

Coat the ribs evenly on both sides with half the sauce. Marinate the ribs, refrigerated, for at least 15 minutes. For more flavor, marinate for up to 8 hours. Reserve the remaining sauce to serve as a sauce for the ribs.

To grill the ribs, if using a gas barbecue, preheat to medium (325°). If using charcoal or wood, prepare a fire. Grill according to the instructions on page 22. Occasionally during cooking, baste the ribs with the marinade, stopping 15 minutes before removing the ribs from the grill.

To smoke the ribs, see page 27. To roast the ribs, see page 29.

To serve, cut each side of ribs in half, into 3 sections, or into individual ribs. Transfer to a heated serving platter or 4 heated dinner plates and serve at once accompanied by the reserved sauce.

Southwest Barbecued Ribs

Serves 4

2 sides spareribs or your favorite ribs

SOUTHWEST BARBECUE SAUCE

4 ancho chiles

1 teaspoon whole allspice

1 teaspoon coriander seeds

1-inch piece cinnamon

$1/2$ teaspoon whole cloves

4 cloves garlic, very finely minced

1 shallot, skin removed

3 serrano chiles, stemmed

1 teaspoon finely grated lime zest

1 teaspoon finely grated orange zest

$1/2$ cup chopped fresh cilantro sprigs

1 cup freshly squeezed orange juice

$1/4$ cup olive oil

2 tablespoons Worcestershire sauce

2 tablespoons honey

2 tablespoons thin soy sauce

Remove the membrane from the underside of the ribs as shown on page 19. Then place the ribs in a rectangular dish or baking pan. To make the barbecue sauce, place the ancho chiles in a bowl and cover them with boiling water. Place a small saucer on the chiles to submerge them. After 30 minutes, stem the chiles and wash away the seeds. Place the allspice, coriander, cinnamon, and cloves in an electric spice grinder and grind them to a powder. In a food processor fitted with the metal blade and a feed tube, mince the garlic, shallot, and chiles. Add the ancho chiles and finely mince. Add all the remaining ingredients and process until completely smooth. Makes 2 $3/4$ cups.

Coat the ribs evenly on both sides with half the sauce. Marinate the ribs, refrigerated, for at least 15 minutes. For more flavor, marinate the ribs for up to 8 hours. Reserve the remaining barbecue sauce to serve as a sauce for the ribs.

To grill the ribs, if using a gas barbecue, preheat to medium (325°). If using charcoal or wood, prepare a fire. Grill according to the instructions on page 22. Occasionally during cooking, baste the ribs with extra marinade, stopping 15 minutes before removing the ribs from the grill.

To smoke the ribs, see page 27. To roast the ribs, see page 29.

To serve, cut each side of ribs in half, into 3 sections, or into individual ribs. Transfer to a heated serving platter or 4 heated dinner plates and serve at once accompanied by the sauce.

Toasting coriander seeds and black peppercorns before grinding them enhances their flavor for chile, molasses, and ketchup based sauces. When toasting the spices it's important that the frying pan be completely grease-free or the spices will not powder when ground. If you don't have an electric spice grinder or a coffee grinder you're willing to spare for this step, then grind the coriander and pepper using a mortar and pestle. We've even used the end of a knife handle to crush the spices.

Chipotle-Coriander Cured Ribs

Serves 4

6 pounds beef ribs or your favorite type of ribs

CHIPOTLE-CORIANDER CURE

$1/4$ cup coriander seeds

$1/4$ cup black peppercorns

8 cloves garlic, peeled

4 shallots, peeled

$1/4$ cup chipotle chiles in adobo sauce

1 cup ketchup

6 tablespoons dark brown sugar

$1/4$ cup molasses

$1/4$ cup dark soy sauce

$1/4$ cup cider vinegar

1 tablespoon finely minced orange zest

Remove the membrane from the underside of the ribs as shown on page 19. Then place the ribs in a rectangular dish or baking pan.

To make the cure, place the coriander seeds and peppercorns in a small sauté pan placed over medium heat and toast until the peppercorns begin to smoke. Transfer to a spice grinder and grind finely. Mince the garlic and shallots in a food processor. Add the ground spices and chipotle chiles and mince for 10 seconds. Add all the remaining ingredients and process until the mixture becomes a thick paste. Makes 2 1/2 cups.

Coat the ribs on both sides with the cure. Marinate the ribs, refrigerated, for at least 15 minutes. For more flavor, marinate for up to 8 hours.

To grill the ribs, if using a gas barbecue, preheat to medium (325°). If using charcoal or wood, prepare a fire. Grill according to the instructions on page 22. Occasionally during cooking, baste the ribs with extra Chipotle-Coriander Cure, stopping 15 minutes before removing the ribs from the grill.

To smoke the ribs, see page 27. To roast the ribs, see page 29.

To serve, cut each side of ribs in half, into 3 sections, or into individual ribs. Transfer to a heated serving platter or 4 heated dinner plates and serve at once.

Mediterranean
and Caribbean
Ribs

Spareribs with Mustard, Garlic, and Rosemary Marinade

Serves 4

2 sides spareribs or your favorite ribs

MUSTARD, GARLIC, AND ROSEMARY MARINADE

$^1/_4$ cup chopped fresh rosemary

$^1/_4$ cup minced shallots

5 cloves garlic, finely minced

10 juniper berries, ground

1 tablespoon minced lemon zest

$^1/_2$ cup dry vermouth

$^1/_3$ cup freshly squeezed lemon juice

$^1/_3$ cup Dijon mustard

$^1/_3$ cup thin soy sauce

$^1/_4$ cup honey

3 tablespoons extra virgin olive oil

2 teaspoons Asian chile sauce

Remove the membrane from the underside of the ribs as shown on page 19. Then place the ribs in a rectangular dish or baking pan.

To make the marinade, combine all the marinade ingredients and stir well. Makes 2 $^1/_2$ cups.

Coat the ribs evenly on both sides with the marinade. Marinate the ribs, refrigerated, for at least 15 minutes. For more flavor, marinate for up to 8 hours.

To grill the ribs, if using a gas barbecue, preheat to medium (325°). If using charcoal or wood, prepare a fire. Grill according to the instructions on page 22. Occasionally during cooking, baste the ribs with extra marinade, stopping 15 minutes before removing the ribs from the grill.

To smoke the ribs, see page 27. To roast the ribs, see page 29.

To serve, cut each side of ribs in half, into 3 sections, or into individual ribs. Transfer to a heated serving platter or 4 heated dinner plates and serve at once.

For a fusion marinade, the rich flavor of hoisin sauce and the intense fruitiness of plum sauce make a perfect match for the spiciness of mustard, fruity sourness of fresh lemon juice, heat from chiles, and the wonderful floral taste contributed by chopped fresh rosemary. Don't compromise and use store-bought lemon juice or dried rosemary. The marinade simply won't taste as good.

Rosemary, Chile, and Hoisin Ribs

Serves 4

2 sides spareribs or your favorite ribs

ROSEMARY, CHILE, AND HOISIN GLAZE

$^1/_2$ cup hoisin sauce
$^1/_2$ cup plum sauce
$^1/_2$ cup dry red wine
$^1/_4$ cup Dijon mustard
$^1/_4$ cup freshly squeezed lemon juice
6 cloves garlic, finely minced
4 serrano chiles, stemmed and finely minced, including the seeds
$^1/_3$ cup fresh rosemary
$^1/_4$ cup chopped fresh sage

Remove the membrane from the underside of the ribs as shown on page 19. Then place the ribs in a rectangular dish or baking pan.

To make the glaze, combine all the glaze ingredients and stir well. Makes 2 $^1/_2$ cups.

Coat the ribs evenly on both sides with the glaze. Marinate the ribs, refrigerated, for at least 15 minutes. For more flavor, marinate for up to 8 hours.

To grill the ribs, if using a gas barbecue, preheat to medium (325°). If using charcoal or wood, prepare a fire. Grill according to the instructions on page 22. Occasionally during cooking, baste the ribs with extra glaze, stopping 15 minutes before removing the ribs from the grill.

To smoke the ribs, see page 27. To roast the ribs, see page 29.

To serve, cut each side of ribs in half, into 3 sections, or into individual ribs. Transfer to a heated serving platter or 4 heated dinner plates and serve at once.

Middle Eastern Ribs with Spicy Pomegranate Glaze

Serves 4

2 sides spareribs or your favorite ribs
2 tablespoons white sesame seeds
$^1/_4$ cup chopped parsley, for garnish
1 teaspoon grated orange zest, for garnish

SPICY POMEGRANATE GLAZE

1 cup pomegranate "molasses" (concentrated juice)
$^1/_4$ cup oyster sauce
2 tablespoons honey
1 tablespoon ground coriander
2 teaspoons crushed red pepper flakes
2 tablespoons finely minced ginger
$^1/_4$ cup minced green onion, green and white parts
$^1/_4$ cup chopped fresh cilantro sprigs

Remove the membrane from the underside of the ribs as shown on page 19. Then place the ribs in a rectangular dish or baking pan.

In an ungreased skillet over high heat, toast the sesame seeds until golden. Set aside.

To make the glaze, combine all the glaze ingredients and stir well. Makes 1 $^1/_2$ cups.

Coat the ribs evenly on both sides with the glaze. Marinate the ribs, refrigerated, for at least 15 minutes. For more flavor, marinate for up to 8 hours.

To grill the ribs, if using a gas barbecue, preheat to medium (325°). If using charcoal or wood, prepare a fire. Grill according to the instructions on page 22. Occasionally during cooking, baste the ribs, stopping 15 minutes before removing the ribs from the grill.

To smoke the ribs, see page 27. To roast the ribs, see page 29.

To serve, cut each side of ribs in half, into 3 sections, or into individual ribs. Transfer to a heated serving platter or 4 heated dinner plates. Sprinkle with the parsley, orange zest, and sesame seeds. Serve at once.

Pork Baby Back Ribs with Jamaican Jerk Marinade

Serves 4

2 sides pork baby back ribs or your favorite type of ribs

JERK MARINADE

$1/2$ cup dark soy sauce

$1/4$ cup distilled white vinegar

$1/4$ cup honey

$1/4$ cup olive oil

1 tablespoon ground coriander

1 tablespoon freshly ground black pepper

2 teaspoons freshly ground nutmeg

2 teaspoons ground allspice

1 teaspoon ground cinnamon

$1/2$ cup chopped cilantro sprigs

$1/2$ cup minced green onions, green and white parts

1 tablespoon minced fresh thyme leaves

10 cloves garlic, finely minced

$1/4$ cup finely minced ginger

3 Scotch bonnet chiles, or 6 very finely minced serrano chiles, including seeds, or 2 tablespoons chile sauce

Remove the membrane from the underside of the ribs as shown on page 19. Then place the ribs in a rectangular dish or baking pan.

To make the marinade, combine all the marinade ingredients and stir well. Makes 2 $3/4$ cups.

Coat the ribs evenly on both sides with the marinade. Marinate the ribs, refrigerated, for at least 15 minutes. For more flavor, marinate for up to 8 hours.

To grill the ribs, if using a gas barbecue, preheat to medium (325°). If using charcoal or wood, prepare a fire. Grill according to the instructions on page 22. Occasionally during cooking, baste the ribs with extra marinade, stopping 15 minutes before removing the ribs from the grill.

To smoke the ribs, see page 27. To roast the ribs, see page 29.

To serve, cut each side of ribs in half, into 3 sections, or into individual ribs. Transfer to a heated serving platter or 4 heated dinner plates and serve at once.

East-West
Lemon-Glazed Ribs

Serves 4

2 sides spareribs or your favorite ribs

EAST-WEST MARINADE

8 cloves garlic, finely minced

1/4 cup minced shallots

2 tablespoons finely minced ginger

Zest from 2 lemons, minced

Juice from 2 lemons

1/3 cup extra virgin olive oil

1/3 cup hoisin sauce

1/3 cup Dijon mustard

1 tablespoon Asian chile sauce

1/4 cup chopped basil leaves or cilantro sprigs

1/4 cup chopped parsley

Remove the membrane from the underside of the ribs as shown on page 19. Then place the ribs in a rectangular dish or baking pan.

To make the marinade, combine all the marinade ingredients and stir well. Makes 2 1/4 cups.

Coat the ribs evenly on both sides with the marinade. Marinate the ribs, refrigerated, for at least 15 minutes. For more flavor, marinate for up to 8 hours.

To grill the ribs, if using a gas barbecue, preheat to medium (325°). If using charcoal or wood, prepare a fire. Grill according to the instructions on page 22. Occasionally during cooking, baste the ribs with extra marinade, stopping 15 minutes before removing the ribs from the grill.

To smoke the ribs, see page 27. To roast the ribs, see page 29.

To serve, cut each side of ribs in half, into 3 sections, or into individual ribs. Transfer to a heated serving platter or 4 heated dinner plates and serve at once.

Moroccan Glazed Ribs

Serves 4

2 sides spareribs or your favorite ribs

MOROCCAN GLAZE

Zest from 2 lemons, finely minced
$^1/_2$ cup freshly squeezed lemon juice
$^1/_4$ cup honey
3 tablespoons extra virgin olive oil
1 tablespoon ground coriander
1 tablespoon ground cumin
1 tablespoon freshly grated nutmeg
2 teaspoons sweet paprika
2 to 3 teaspoons cayenne or crushed red pepper flakes
1 teaspoon salt
6 cloves garlic, finely minced
2 green onions, green and white parts, finely minced
$^1/_2$ cup chopped cilantro sprigs
$^1/_2$ cup chopped mint leaves

Remove the membrane from the underside of the ribs as shown on page 19. Then place the ribs in a rectangular dish or baking pan.

To make the glaze, combine all the glaze ingredients and stir well. Makes 2 cups.

Coat the ribs evenly on both sides with the glaze. Marinate the ribs, refrigerated, for at least 15 minutes. For more flavor, marinate for up to 8 hours.

To grill the ribs, if using a gas barbecue, preheat to medium (325°). If using charcoal or wood, prepare a fire. Grill according to the instructions on page 22. Occasionally during cooking, baste the ribs with extra glaze, stopping 15 minutes before removing the ribs from the grill.

To smoke the ribs, see page 27. To roast the ribs, see page 29.

To serve, cut each side of ribs in half, into 3 sections, or into individual ribs. Transfer to a heated serving platter or 4 heated dinner plates and serve at once.

The combination of soy sauce and powdered mustard is a classic Cantonese dipping sauce. This recipe draws from this idea by substituting honey mustard and adding ground spices, chiles, and garlic. If you don't have honey mustard, any good Dijon-style French mustard will work fine. Variations we've enjoyed include adding 2 tablespoons of chopped fresh rosemary and 1 tablespoon of finely minced ginger.

Spicy Honey Mustard Ribs

Serves 4

2 pounds country-style spareribs (with bone) or your favorite ribs

1 cup honey mustard

$1/4$ cup thin soy sauce

2 tablespoons honey

1 tablespoon chile sauce, extra spicy

2 teaspoons ground cumin

2 teaspoons ground cinnamon

4 cloves garlic, finely minced

Remove the membrane from the underside of the ribs as shown on page 19. Then place the ribs in a rectangular dish or baking pan.

To make the rub, combine all the rub ingredients and stir well. Makes 1 $1/2$ cups.

Coat the ribs evenly on both sides with the rub. Marinate the ribs, refrigerated, for at least 15 minutes. For more flavor, marinate for up to 8 hours.

To grill the ribs, if using a gas barbecue, preheat to medium (325°). If using charcoal or wood, prepare a fire. Grill according to the instructions on page 22. Occasionally during cooking, baste the ribs with extra marinade, stopping 15 minutes before removing the ribs from the grill.

To smoke the ribs, see page 27. To roast the ribs, see page 29.

To serve, cut each side of ribs in half, into 3 sections, or into individual ribs. Transfer to a heated serving platter or 4 heated dinner plates and serve at once.

Balsamic Vinegar, Soy, and Honey Mustard Ribs

Serves 4

2 sides of spareribs or your favorite ribs
1 1/2 teaspoon red peppercorns
1 1/2 teaspoon green peppercorns
1 1/2 teaspoon white peppercorns
1 1/2 teaspoon black peppercorns
1/2 cup Swedish mustard or honey mustard

BALSAMIC MOP
6 tablespoons balsamic vinegar
6 tablespoons dry red wine
1/4 cup dark soy sauce
1/4 cup Dijon mustard
5 cloves garlic, finely minced

Remove the membrane from the underside of the ribs as shown on page 19. Then place the ribs in a rectangular dish or baking pan.

Place the peppercorns in a sauté pan over medium heat and toast them until they begin to pop and hop. Transfer the peppercorns to a spice grinder or mortar and pestle and coarsely grind them. Combine the ground peppercorns with the mustard.

Using your fingers or a spoon, rub the mustard and pepper over the ribs, coating them evenly. Marinate the ribs, refrigerated, for at least 15 minutes. For more flavor, marinate for up to 8 hours.

To make the mop, combine all the mop ingredients in a small bowl. Stir well and set aside.

To grill the ribs, if using a gas barbecue, preheat to medium (325°). If using charcoal or wood, prepare a fire. Grill according to the instructions on page 22. During grilling, gently brush the ribs with the mop, stopping 15 minutes before removing the ribs from the grill.

To smoke the ribs, see page 27. To roast the ribs, see page 29.

To serve, cut each side of ribs in half, into 3 sections, or into individual ribs. Transfer to a heated serving platter or 4 heated dinner plates and serve at once.

Tuscan-Style Barbecued Ribs

Serves 4

2 sides spareribs or your favorite ribs
1 teaspoon grated orange zest
1 teaspoon grated lemon zest

TUSCAN MARINADE

1 head garlic
$1/4$ cup plus 1 tablespoon extra virgin olive oil
1 tablespoon minced lemon zest
$1/3$ cup freshly squeezed lemon juice
2 tablespoons honey
$1/3$ cup pitted kamalata olives, minced
2 tablespoons chopped fresh rosemary
2 tablespoons anchovy paste
1 teaspoon crushed red pepper flakes

Remove the membrane from the underside of the ribs as shown on page 19. Then place the ribs in a rectangular dish or baking pan.

To make the marinade, preheat the oven to 400°. Trim the top of the head of garlic, exposing the tips of the cloves, and drizzle 1 tablespoon olive oil over the head of garlic. Wrap it in foil, and bake it for 1 hour. Then squeeze the garlic from the cloves and mash it with a fork. In a bowl, combine the garlic and all the remaining marinade ingredients. Stir well. Makes 1 cup.

Coat the ribs evenly on both sides with the marinade. Marinate the ribs, refrigerated, for at least 15 minutes. For more flavor, marinate for up to 8 hours.

To grill the ribs, if using a gas barbecue, preheat to medium (325°). If using charcoal or wood, prepare a fire. Grill according to the instructions on page 22. Occasionally during cooking, baste the ribs with extra marinade, stopping 15 minutes before removing the ribs from the grill.

To smoke the ribs, see page 27. To roast the ribs, see page 29.

To serve, cut each side of ribs in half, into 3 sections, or into individual ribs. Transfer to a heated serving platter or 4 heated dinner plates. Sprinkle the ribs with the orange and lemon zest and serve at once.

Fruit-Based Barbecue Glazes

Ribs Crusted with Apricot Glaze

Serves 4

2 sides pork baby back ribs or your favorite ribs

SPICY APRICOT GLAZE

16 dried apricots
1 1/2 cups apricot nectar
3/4 cup sugar
1/2 cup white distilled vinegar
1/2 cup water
1 to 2 tablespoons Asian chile sauce
1 teaspoon salt
1/3 cup finely minced ginger
3 cloves garlic, minced
2 tablespoons white sesame seeds
2 green onions, green and white parts, minced
1/4 cup minced cilantro sprigs

Remove the membrane from the underside of the ribs as shown on page 19. Then place the ribs in a rectangular dish or baking pan.

To make the glaze, in a small nonreactive saucepan, combine the apricots, nectar, sugar, vinegar, water, chile sauce, salt, ginger, and garlic. Bring to a low boil, reduce the heat to a simmer, cover, and cook for 30 minutes. Allow to cool to room temperature. Then purée in an electric blender until completely smooth. Transfer to a bowl.

Place the sesame seeds in an ungreased skillet and toast over medium heat until golden. Add the sesame seeds, green onion, and cilantro to the apricot glaze. Makes 3 3/4 cups.

Coat the ribs evenly on both sides with half the glaze. Marinate the ribs, refrigerated, for at least 15 minutes. For more flavor, marinate for up to 8 hours. Reserve the remaining glaze to use as a sauce for the ribs.

To grill the ribs, if using a gas barbecue, preheat to medium (325°). If using charcoal or wood, prepare a fire. Grill according to the instructions on page 22. Occasionally during cooking, baste the ribs with the marinade, stopping 15 minutes before removing the ribs from the grill.

To smoke the ribs, see page 27. To roast the ribs, see page 29.

To serve, cut each side of ribs in half, into 3 sections, or into individual ribs. Transfer to a heated serving platter or 4 heated dinner plates and serve at once accompanied by the reserved sauce.

Raspberry jam or any other jam combined with vinegar, soy, chiles, and ginger makes a delicious glaze to brush across ribs. Because raspberry jam burns easily, cook the ribs over a medium fire or in a 325° oven, and don't baste with extra marinade until the last 20 minutes of cooking.

Sweet-and-Sour Raspberry-Glazed Ribs

Serves 4

2 sides spareribs or your favorite ribs

SWEET-AND-SOUR RASPBERRY GLAZE

2 tablespoons white sesame seeds

$1/2$ cup raspberry jam

$1/2$ cup wine vinegar

$1/4$ cup dark soy sauce

$1/4$ cup finely minced ginger

2 teaspoons chile sauce

$1/4$ cup minced green onion, green and white parts

$1/2$ teaspoon Chinese five-spice powder or cinnamon

Remove the membrane from the underside of the ribs as shown on page 19. Then place the ribs in a rectangular dish or baking pan.

To make the glaze, in an ungreased skillet over high heat toast the sesame seeds until golden. Transfer the seeds to a bowl and combine with the remaining glaze ingredients. Stir well. Makes 1 $1/2$ cups.

Coat the ribs evenly on both sides with the glaze. Marinate the ribs, refrigerated, for at least 15 minutes. For more flavor, marinate for up to 8 hours.

To grill the ribs, if using a gas barbecue, preheat to medium (325°). If using charcoal or wood, prepare a fire. Grill according to the instructions on page 22. Occasionally during cooking, baste the ribs with extra glaze, stopping 15 minutes before removing the ribs from the grill.

To smoke the ribs, see page 27. To roast the ribs, see page 29.

To serve, cut each side of ribs in half, into 3 sections, or into individual ribs. Transfer to a heated serving platter or 4 heated dinner plates and serve at once.

FRUIT-BASED BARBECUE GLAZES

Spicy Orange-Glazed Ribs

Serves 4

2 sides lamb riblets or your favorite ribs

$^1/_4$ cup white sesame seeds
$^1/_2$ cup orange juice concentrate
$^1/_4$ cup orange marmalade
$^1/_4$ cup honey
$^1/_4$ cup wine vinegar
1 tablespoon Asian chile sauce
2 cloves garlic, finely minced
$^1/_4$ cup finely minced ginger
$^1/_4$ cup minced green onion, green and white parts
2 tablespoons minced orange zest

Remove the membrane from the underside of the ribs as shown on page 19. Then place the ribs in a rectangular dish or baking pan.

To make the glaze, in an ungreased skillet over high heat, toast the sesame seeds until golden. Transfer the seeds to a bowl and combine with the remaining glaze ingredients. Stir well. Makes 3 cups.

Coat the ribs evenly on both sides with half the glaze. Marinate the ribs, refrigerated, for at least 15 minutes. For more flavor, marinate for up to 8 hours. Reserve the remaining glaze to serve as a sauce for the ribs.

To grill the ribs, if using a gas barbecue, preheat to medium (325°). If using charcoal or wood, prepare a fire. Grill according to the instructions on page 22. Occasionally during cooking, baste the ribs with the marinade, stopping 15 minutes before removing the ribs from the grill.

To smoke the ribs, see page 27. To roast the ribs, see page 29.

To serve, cut each side of ribs in half, into 3 sections, or into individual ribs. Transfer to a heated serving platter or 4 heated dinner plates and serve at once, accompanied by the reserved sauce.

Spicy Cherry-Glazed Ribs

Serves 4

2 sides pork baby back ribs or your favorite ribs

$1/4$ cup brown sugar
2 tablespoons chile powder
2 teaspoons ground nutmeg
2 teaspoons ground coriander
2 teaspoons dry sage
2 teaspoons dry oregano

SPICY CHERRY GLAZE
$1/2$ cup black cherry jam
$1/2$ cup wine vinegar
1 teaspoon crushed red pepper flakes
2 tablespoons finely minced ginger
2 cloves garlic, finely minced

Remove the membrane from the underside of the ribs as shown on page 19. Then place the ribs in a rectangular dish or baking dish.

To make the rub, combine the dry rub ingredients. Using your fingers, vigorously rub the dry rub on both sides of the ribs. Marinate the ribs, refrigerated, for at least 15 minutes. For more flavor, marinate for up to 24 hours.

To make the glaze, in a small bowl, combine the glaze ingredients. Stir well.

To grill the ribs, if using a gas barbecue, preheat to medium (325°). If using charcoal or wood, prepare a fire. Grill according to the instructions on page 22. Baste the ribs with the glaze only during the last 30 minutes or grilling or the glaze will burn.

To smoke the ribs, see page 27. Brush with the cherry glaze during the last 30 minutes of smoking.

To roast the ribs, see page 29. Occasionally during roasting, baste with the glaze.

To serve, cut each side of ribs in half, into 3 sections, or into individual ribs. Transfer to a heated serving platter or 4 heated dinner plates and serve at once accompanied by extra cherry glaze in a bowl.

Ribs with Thai Mango Sauce

Serves 4

2 sides spareribs or your favorite ribs

THAI MANGO SAUCE

1 cup mango purée, about 2 ripe mangoes

$1/4$ cup Thai or Vietnamese fish sauce

$1/4$ cup freshly squeezed lime juice

$1/4$ cup light brown sugar

2 tablespoons flavorless cooking oil

1 tablespoon Asian chile sauce

2 tablespoons finely minced ginger

3 cloves garlic, finely minced

$1/4$ cup chopped cilantro sprigs

Remove the membrane from the underside of the ribs as described on page 19. Then place the ribs in a rectangular dish or baking pan.

To make the sauce, peel the mangoes and cut the flesh away from the seed. Place the mango flesh in a food processor fitted with a metal blade and purée. Transfer the mango purée to a bowl and combine with the remaining sauce ingredients. Stir well. Makes 1 $3/4$ cups.

Coat the ribs evenly on both sides with half the sauce. Marinate the ribs, refrigerated, for at least 15 minutes. For more flavor, marinate for up to 8 hours. Reserve the remaining sauce to serve as a sauce for the ribs.

To grill the ribs, if using a gas barbecue, preheat to medium (325°). If using charcoal or wood, prepare a fire. Grill according to the instructions on page 22. Occasionally during cooking, baste the ribs with the marinade, stopping 15 minutes before removing the ribs from the grill.

To smoke the ribs, see page 27. To roast the ribs, see page 29.

To serve, cut each side of ribs in half, into 3 sections, or into individual ribs. Transfer to a heated serving platter or 4 heated dinner plates and serve at once accompanied by the reserved sauce.

FRUIT-BASED BARBECUE GLAZES

How British with marmalade—how shocking with ancho chiles, soy sauce, and cilantro! But the combination of sweet, sour, spicy, and herbal flavors creates a dynamic contrast with each bite. If you want to make the marinade more than two days ahead, omit the green onions and cilantro. Then the marinade can be made in a large amount and kept indefinitely in the refrigerator. When you want to use the marinade, just pour the amount you need and add the freshly chopped green onions and cilantro.

Ribs with Ancho Marmalade Rub

Serves 4

2 sides pork baby back ribs or your favorite ribs

ANCHO MARMALADE RUB

4 ancho chiles

$^1/_2$ cup orange marmalade

$^1/_2$ cup wine vinegar

$^1/_4$ cup dark soy sauce

$^1/_4$ cup olive oil

1 tablespoon Asian chile sauce

$^1/_4$ cup finely minced ginger

$^1/_4$ cup minced green onions, green and white parts

$^1/_4$ cup chopped cilantro sprigs

Remove the membrane from the underside of the ribs as shown on page 19. Then place the ribs in a rectangular dish or baking pan.

To make the rub, place the ancho chiles in a bowl and cover with boiling water. Place a small saucer on the chiles to submerge them. After 30 minutes, stem the chiles and wash away the seeds. Transfer the chiles to an electric blender and add the marmalade, vinegar, soy sauce, olive oil, chile sauce, and ginger. Liquefy. Transfer to a bowl. Stir in the green onions and cilantro. Makes 1 $^3/_4$ cups.

Coat the ribs evenly on both sides with half the rub. Marinate the ribs, refrigerated, for at least 15 minutes. For more flavor, marinate for up to 8 hours. Reserve remaining rub to serve as a sauce for the ribs.

To grill the ribs, if using a gas barbecue, preheat to medium (325°). If using charcoal or wood, prepare a fire. Grill according to the instructions on page 22. Occasionally during cooking, baste the ribs with the marinade, stopping 15 minutes before removing the ribs from the grill.

To smoke the ribs, see page 27. To roast the ribs, see page 29.

To serve, cut each side of ribs in half, into 3 sections, or into individual ribs. Transfer the ribs to a heated serving platter or 4 heated dinner plates and serve them at once, accompanied by the reserved sauce.

FRUIT-BASED BARBECUE GLAZES

Strawberry-Habanero Marinated Ribs

Serves 4

2 sides spareribs or your favorite ribs

STRAWBERRY-HABANERO MARINADE
$1/2$ cup strawberry jam
Zest of 2 limes, grated or finely minced
Juice of 2 limes
$1/4$ cup thin soy sauce
2 tablespoons habanero hot sauce
$1/4$ cup finely minced ginger
$1/4$ cup minced mint leaves

Remove the membrane from the underside of the ribs as shown on page 19. Then place the ribs in a rectangular dish or baking pan.

To make the marinade, combine all the marinade ingredients. Stir well. Makes 1 $1/4$ cups.

Coat the ribs evenly on both sides with the marinade. Marinate the ribs, refrigerated, for at least 15 minutes. For more flavor, marinate for up to 8 hours.

To grill the ribs, if using a gas barbecue, preheat to medium (325°). If using charcoal or wood, prepare a fire. Grill according to the instructions on page 22. Occasionally during cooking, baste the ribs with extra marinade, stopping 15 minutes before removing the ribs from the grill.

To smoke the ribs, see page 27. To roast the ribs, see page 29.

To serve, cut each side of ribs in half, into 3 sections, or into individual ribs. Transfer to a heated serving platter or 4 heated dinner plates and serve at once.

Dried fruit makes a great flavor base for a marinade. Figs are softened in hot water (you can substitute dates or dried apricots) and then puréed with a little of the soaking water. The sweet, rich flavor of a fruit purée is more than a match for equally rich hoisin sauce. Adding ground spices and chiles adds the necessary flavor contrasts to give this marinade its complex taste.

Ribs with Spicy Fig Glaze

Serves 4

2 sides spareribs or your favorite ribs

SPICY FIG GLAZE

12 dried figs

$^1/_2$ cup hoisin sauce

$^1/_2$ cup freshly squeezed orange juice

$^1/_4$ cup wine vinegar

$^1/_4$ cup olive oil

1 tablespoon chile sauce

$^1/_2$ teaspoon allspice

$^1/_2$ teaspoon cinnamon

4 cloves garlic, finely minced

$^1/_4$ cup finely minced ginger

$^1/_4$ cup minced green onions, green and white parts

Remove the membrane from the underside of the ribs as shown on page 19. Then place the ribs in a rectangular dish or baking pan.

To make the glaze, place the figs in a bowl and cover them with 1 cup of boiling water. After 30 minutes, place the figs, $^1/_4$ cup of the water, and all the remaining glaze ingredients except the green onions in an electric blender. Blend into a liquid. Transfer to a bowl and add the green onions. Makes 1 $^1/_2$ cups.

Coat the ribs evenly on both sides with the marinade. Marinate the ribs, refrigerated, for at least 15 minutes. For more flavor, marinate for up to 8 hours.

To grill the ribs, if using a gas barbecue, preheat to medium (325°). If using charcoal or wood, prepare a fire. Grill according to the instructions on page 22. Occasionally during cooking, baste the ribs with extra glaze, stopping 15 minutes before removing the ribs from the grill.

To smoke the ribs, see page 27. To roast the ribs, see page 29.

To serve, cut each side of ribs in half, into 3 sections, or into individual ribs. Transfer to a heated serving platter or 4 heated dinner plates and serve at once.

Ribs with Fiery Mango Marinade

Serves 4

6 pounds beef ribs or your favorite ribs

1 large fresh ripe mango
2 tablespoons chipotle chiles in adobo sauce
$1/4$ cup ketchup
$1/4$ cup tequila
$1/4$ cup freshly squeezed lime juice
2 tablespoons oyster sauce
2 tablespoons honey
6 cloves garlic, finely minced
$1/4$ cup finely minced ginger
$1/4$ cup chopped cilantro sprigs

Remove the membrane from the underside of the ribs as shown on page 19. Then place the ribs in a rectangular dish or baking pan.

To make the marinade, peel the mango and cut the flesh away from the seed. Combine the mango flesh and chipotle chiles in a food processor fitted with a metal blade and purée. Transfer the mixture to a bowl and combine with the remaining marinade ingredients. Makes 2 cups.

Coat the ribs evenly on both sides with half the marinade. Marinate the ribs, refrigerated, for at least 15 minutes. For more flavor, marinate for up to 8 hours. Reserve the remaining marinade to serve as a sauce for the ribs.

To grill the ribs, if using a gas barbecue, preheat to medium (325°). If using charcoal or wood, prepare a fire. Grill according to the instructions on page 22. Occasionally during cooking, baste the ribs with extra marinade, stopping 15 minutes before removing the ribs from the grill.

To smoke the ribs, see page 27. To roast the ribs, see page 29.

To serve, cut each side of ribs in half, into 3 sections, or into individual ribs. Transfer to a heated serving platter or 4 heated dinner plates and serve at once accompanied by the reserved sauce.

Ribs with Spicy Caribbean Pineapple Marinade

Serves 4

2 sides spareribs or your favorite ribs

SPICY CARIBBEAN PINEAPPLE MARINADE
$^1/_2$ fresh pineapple
$^1/_4$ cup flavorless cooking oil
$^1/_4$ cup light brown sugar
$^1/_4$ cup thin soy sauce
1 tablespoon curry powder
1 teaspoon ground allspice
$^1/_4$ cup finely minced ginger
$^1/_4$ cup minced green onions, green and white parts
$^1/_4$ cup minced cilantro sprigs
4 serrano chiles, finely minced, including the seeds

Remove the membrane from the underside of the ribs as shown on page 19. Then place the ribs in a rectangular dish or baking pan.

To make the marinade, peel and core the pineapple. In a food processor fitted with a metal blade, purée half the pineapple. Transfer the purée to a bowl and chop the remaining pineapple in the food processor. Combine the chopped pineapple and the pineapple purée with the remaining marinade ingredients. Stir well. Makes 3 $^1/_4$ cups.

Coat the ribs on both sides evenly with half the marinade. Marinate the ribs, refrigerated, for at least 15 minutes. For more flavor, marinate for up to 8 hours. Reserve the remaining marinade to serve as a sauce for the ribs.

To grill the ribs, if using a gas barbecue, preheat to medium (325°). If using charcoal or wood, prepare a fire. Grill according to the instructions on page 22. Occasionally during cooking, baste the ribs with extra marinade, stopping 15 minutes before removing the ribs from the grill.

To smoke the ribs, see page 27. To roast the ribs, see page 29.

To serve, cut each side of ribs in half, into 3 sections, or into individual ribs. Transfer to a heated serving platter or 4 heated dinner plates and serve at once accompanied by the reserved sauce.

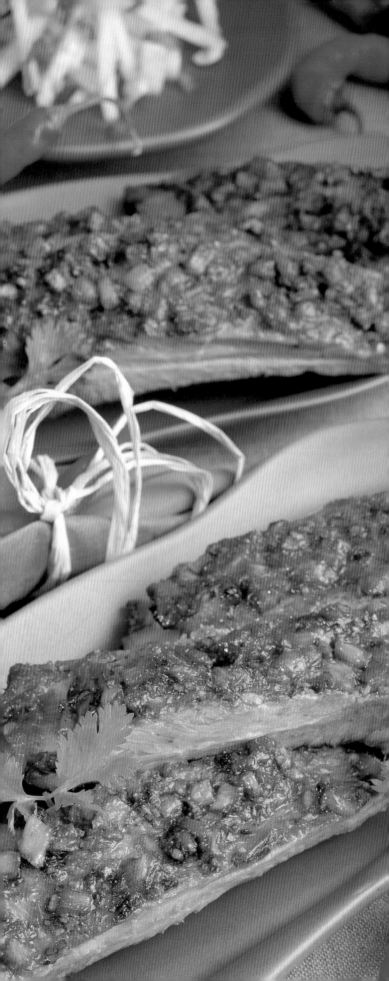

Succulent Braised Ribs

Ribs with Spicy Tomato Glaze

Serves 4

2 pounds beef short ribs or your favorite ribs
$1/4$ cup flavorless cooking oil
$1/4$ cup chopped cilantro sprigs

SPICY TOMATO GLAZE

$1 1/2$ cups best-quality tomato spaghetti sauce
1 cup dry red wine
2 tablespoons oyster sauce
2 tablespoons hoisin sauce
1 tablespoon dark sesame oil
1 tablespoon Asian chile sauce
$1/4$ cup chopped cilantro sprigs
4 cloves garlic, finely minced
2 tablespoons finely minced ginger

Trim all fat from the short ribs. If using pork ribs, ask the butcher to cut the ribs across the bones into 2-inch-wide strips. Peel off the membrane on the underside of the ribs as shown on page 19. Then cut each strip into 6-inch lengths.

To make the glaze, combine all the glaze ingredients in a bowl. Stir well.

To braise the ribs, place a heavy stewpot over medium heat. Add the cooking oil. When the oil gives off little wisps of smoke, add the ribs. Fry the ribs until they are lightly browned. Tip out and discard the oil. Add the glaze to the pot holding the ribs. Bring to a low boil, cover the pot, and decrease the heat to low, so the glaze is at a simmer. Cook the ribs until the meat is tender, about 2 hours for beef and 1 hour for pork. About every 15 minutes during cooking, stir the ribs.

Temporarily remove the ribs from the pot and, using strips of paper towels, lift off all oil that is floating on the surface of the glaze. Return the ribs to the pot and bring to a simmer. If you do not plan to serve the ribs within the hour, they may be refrigerated in the glaze up to 24 hours before returning the ribs to a simmer.

You can keep the ribs warm for up to 1 hour, on lowest heat, before serving. Transfer the ribs to heated dinner plates, sprinkle with cilantro, and serve glazed with the sauce.

Ribs Braised with Soy and Ginger

Serves 4

4 pounds pork baby back ribs (about 2 sides) or your favorite ribs

1 orange

2 cups dry red wine

$1/2$ cup heavy soy sauce

$1/4$ cup brown sugar

2 tablespoons oyster sauce

2 tablespoons hoisin sauce

1 cinnamon stick

10 juniper berries, crushed

6 whole cloves

3 dried red chiles (optional)

$1/4$ cup thinly sliced fresh ginger

10 cloves garlic, peeled and crushed

Ask the butcher to cut the ribs across the bone into 2-inch-wide strips. Remove the membrane from the underside of the ribs, as shown on page 19. Then cut the strips into 6-inch lengths.

To make the braising sauce, in a 4-quart saucepan, remove all the orange skin with a potato peeler. Combine the orange skin with all the remaining ingredients for the sauce. Bring to a boil, cover, decrease the heat to a simmer, and allow the sauce to simmer for 30 minutes.

To braise the ribs, add the ribs to the pot. Cover the pot and simmer until the meat is tender, about 1 hour. Serve at once accompanied by a little of the braising liquid. If you are not serving the ribs immediately, you can turn off the heat and leave the saucepan at room temperature for up to 4 hours. You can also refrigerate the ribs submerged in the sauce for up to a day in advance of serving.

To reheat the ribs, bring the sauce to a simmer and allow the ribs to simmer for 5 minutes.

Spicy Braised Spareribs

Serves 4

4 pounds spareribs (about 2 sides), or your favorite ribs
10 dried shiitake mushrooms
$^1/_4$ cup flavorless cooking oil
1 yellow onion, peeled and chopped
2 tablespoons cornstarch

SAUCE

1 tablespoon minced garlic
1 tablespoon minced ginger
1 cup chicken broth
$^1/_2$ cup tomato sauce
$^1/_4$ cup dry sherry or Chinese rice wine
2 tablespoons hoisin sauce
2 tablespoons thin soy sauce
2 teaspoons dark soy sauce
2 teaspoons Asian chile sauce
$^1/_2$ teaspoon salt

Ask the butcher to cut the ribs across the bone into 2-inch-wide strips. Remove the membrane from the underside of the ribs as shown on page 19. Then cut the strips into 6-inch lengths.

Soak the mushrooms in hot water until they are soft, about 30 minutes. Then discard the stems and cut the mushrooms into $^1/_3$-inch-thick slices.

To make the sauce, combine the sauce ingredients in a small bowl. Stir well.

To braise the ribs, place a heavy stewpot over medium heat. Add the cooking oil. When the oil gives off little wisps of smoke, add the ribs. Fry the ribs until they are lightly browned, about 5 minutes. Tip out and discard the oil. Add the mushrooms, onion, and sauce to the pot holding the ribs. Bring to a low boil, cover the pot, and decrease the heat to low, so the sauce is at a simmer. Cook the ribs until the meat is tender, about 1 hour. About every 15 minutes during cooking, stir the ribs. Temporarily remove the ribs from the pot and, using strips of paper towels, lift off all oil that is floating on the surface of the sauce. Return the ribs to the pot and bring to a simmer. If you do not plan to serve the ribs within the hour, they may be refrigerated in the sauce up to 24 hours before returning them to a simmer.

Mix the cornstarch with an equal amount of cold water. Stir just enough of the cornstarch mixture in with the ribs to lightly thicken the sauce. You can keep the ribs warm for up to 1 hour, on lowest heat, before serving.

Ribs Simmered in Asian Cabernet Sauce

Serves 4

2 pounds country-style spareribs or your favorite ribs
$1/4$ cup olive oil
2 small yellow onions, chopped
1 tablespoon cornstarch
$1/4$ cup chopped cilantro sprigs

ASIAN CABERNET SAUCE

$1/2$ cup dried cèpe (porcini) mushrooms
1 cup chicken broth
4 cloves garlic, finely minced
1 cup cabernet sauvignon or other dry red wine
2 tablespoons oyster sauce
1 tablespoon dark soy sauce
2 teaspoons tomato paste
1 teaspoon Asian chile sauce
$1/2$ teaspoon sugar
$1/4$ teaspoon freshly ground black pepper
1 tablespoon chopped fresh thyme leaves

If using pork baby back ribs or spareribs, ask the butcher to cut them across the bone into 2-inch-wide strips. Remove the membrane from the underside of the ribs, as shown on page 19. Then cut the strips into 6-inch lengths.

To make the sauce, soak the mushrooms in hot chicken broth for 30 minutes. Then chop the softened mushrooms and set aside. Pour the broth through a fine-meshed strainer. In a bowl, combine the broth with all remaining sauce ingredients. Stir well.

To braise the ribs, place a heavy stewpot over medium heat. Add the olive oil. When the oil gives off little wisps of smoke, add the ribs. Fry the ribs until they are lightly browned, about 5 minutes. Temporarily remove the ribs, and add the onion. Sauté the onions until they brown, about 10 minutes. Then return the meat to the pot and add the mushrooms and the sauce. Bring to a low boil, cover the pot, and decrease the heat to low, so the sauce is at a simmer. Cook the ribs until the meat is tender, about 1 hour. About every 15 minutes during cooking, stir the ribs.

Temporarily remove the ribs from the pot and, using strips of paper towels, lift off all oil that is floating on the surface of the sauce. Return the ribs to the pot and bring to a simmer for 5 minutes to heat through. If you do not plan to serve the ribs within the hour, they may be refrigerated in the sauce up to 24 hours before returning the ribs to a simmer.

Chop the cilantro. Place the ribs on a serving platter or dinner plates. Strain the sauce through a sieve. Return the sauce to the pan and bring to a low boil. Mix the cornstarch with an equal amount of cold water. Stir in just enough of the cornstarch mixture to lightly thicken the sauce. Taste and adjust the seasonings, especially for salt and pepper. Pour the sauce over the ribs, sprinkle with cilantro, and serve.

Ribs in Spicy Coconut Herb Sauce

Serves 4

2 sides pork baby back ribs or your favorite ribs
$1/4$ cup cooking oil
1 tablespoon cornstarch
2 tablespoons chopped cilantro sprigs
2 tablespoons chopped mint leaves

SPICY COCONUT HERB SAUCE
4 cloves garlic, finely minced
2 tablespoons finely minced ginger
1 cup coconut milk, unsweetened
$1/2$ cup freshly squeezed orange juice
2 tablespoons Thai or Vietnamese fish sauce
2 tablespoons Chinese rice wine or dry sherry
Zest from 1 lime, finely minced
1 teaspoon chile sauce
1 teaspoon curry powder
$1/2$ teaspoon allspice

Ask the butcher to cut the ribs across the bone, into 2-inch-wide strips. Remove the membrane from the underside of the ribs, as shown on page 19. Then cut each strip into 6-inch lengths.

To make the sauce, combine the sauce ingredients in a small bowl. Stir well.

To braise the ribs, place a heavy stewpot over medium heat. Add the cooking oil. When the oil gives off little wisps of smoke, add the ribs. Fry the ribs until they are lightly browned, about 5 minutes. Tip out and discard the oil. Add the sauce to the pot holding the ribs. Bring to a low boil, cover the pot, and decrease the heat to low, so the sauce is at a simmer. Cook the ribs until the meat is tender, about 1 hour. About every 15 minutes during cooking, stir the ribs.

Temporarily remove the ribs from the pot and, using strips of paper towels, lift off all oil that is floating on the surface of the sauce. Return the ribs to the pot and bring to a simmer for 5 minutes, to heat through. If you do not plan to serve the ribs within the hour, they may be refrigerated in the sauce up to 24 hours before returning the ribs to a simmer.

Mix the cornstarch with an equal amount of cold water. Stir in just enough of the cornstarch mixture to lightly thicken the sauce. Chop the herbs and stir them into the sauce. You can keep the ribs warm for up to 1 hour, on lowest heat, before serving. Serve the ribs glazed in the sauce.

Chinese salted black beans add flavorful depth to a sauce containing ginger, garlic, and sesame oil. It's important to buy Chinese black beans that are dried and fermented rather than the processed black bean sauce. The latter has an overwhelmingly salty taste. Because black beans are preserved in salt, place them in a sieve and rinse thoroughly before chopping them.

Braised Ribs in Chinese Black Bean Sauce

Serves 4

4 pounds (about 2 sides) pork baby back ribs, or your favorite ribs
$1/4$ cup flavorless cooking oil
4 cloves garlic, finely minced
2 tablespoons finely minced ginger
2 tablespoons salted black beans, rinsed and chopped
1 tablespoon cornstarch

CHINESE BLACK BEAN SAUCE
1 cup chicken broth
$1/2$ cup dry sherry or Chinese rice wine
2 tablespoons thin soy sauce
2 tablespoons hoisin sauce
1 tablespoon dark sesame oil
2 teaspoons Asian chile sauce
2 teaspoons sugar

Ask the butcher to cut the ribs across the bone, into 2-inch-wide strips. Remove the membrane from the underside of the ribs, as shown on page 19. Then cut each strip into 6-inch lengths.

To make the sauce, combine all the sauce ingredients in a small bowl. Stir well.

To braise the ribs, place a heavy stewpot over medium heat. Add the cooking oil. When the oil gives off little wisps of smoke, add the ribs. Fry the ribs until they are lightly browned, about 5 minutes. Tip out and discard the oil. Add the garlic, ginger, and black beans to the pot holding the ribs. Stir and toss with the ribs over medium heat for 30 seconds. Then add the sauce. Bring to a low boil, cover the pot, and decrease the heat to low, so the sauce is at a simmer. Cook the ribs until the meat is tender, about 1 hour. About every 15 minutes during cooking, stir the ribs.

Temporarily remove the ribs from the pot and, using strips of paper towels, lift off all oil that is floating on the surface of the sauce. Return the ribs to the sauce and bring to a simmer for 5 minutes, to heat through. If you do not plan to serve the ribs within the hour, they may be refrigerated in the sauce for up to 24 hours before returning them to a simmer.

Mix the cornstarch with an equal amount of cold water. Stir in just enough of the cornstarch mixture to lightly thicken the sauce. You can keep the ribs warm for up to 1 hour, on lowest heat, before serving. Serve the ribs glazed with the sauce.

New Orleans–Style Glazed Ribs

Serves 4

4 pounds (about 2 sides) pork baby back ribs, or your favorite ribs
$1/4$ cup olive oil
1 cup andouille sausage, chopped
1 yellow onion, chopped
$1/4$ cup chopped parsley

SPICY NEW ORLEANS–STYLE SAUCE

6 cloves garlic, finely minced
Zest from 1 lemon, grated
2 tablespoons chopped fresh oregano leaves
2 tablespoons minced fresh thyme sprigs
$1/2$ green bell pepper, seeded and chopped
2 cups seeded and chopped vine-ripened tomatoes
1 cup heavy whipping cream
$1/2$ cup chicken broth
2 tablespoons Worcestershire sauce
1 tablespoon Asian chile sauce
$1/4$ teaspoon allspice

Ask the butcher to cut the ribs across the bone into 2-inch-wide strips. Remove the membrane from the underside of the ribs, as shown on page 19. Then cut each strip into 6-inch lengths.

To make the sauce, combine the sauce ingredients in a small bowl. Stir well.

To braise the ribs, place a heavy stewpot over medium heat. Add the cooking oil. When the oil give off little wisps of smoke, add the ribs. Fry the ribs until they are lightly browned, about 5 minutes. Remove the ribs temporarily. Add the sausage and onion to the pot. Cook until the onions brown. Then return the ribs, and add the sauce. Bring to a low boil, cover the pot, and decrease the heat to low, so the sauce is at a simmer. Cook the ribs until the meat is tender, about 1 hour. About every 15 minutes during cooking, stir the ribs.

Temporarily remove the ribs from the pot and, using strips of paper towels, lift off all oil that is floating on the surface of the sauce. Strain the sauce through a sieve, and then return the sauce and ribs to the pot and bring to a simmer for 5 minutes, to heat through. If you do not plan to serve the ribs within the hour, they may be refrigerated in the sauce up to 24 hours before returning them to a simmer.

Transfer the ribs to a serving dish. Bring the sauce to a vigorous boil, and boil the sauce over high heat until it thickens enough to lightly coat a spoon, about 5 minutes. Spoon the sauce over the ribs. Sprinkle with parsley and serve.

Ribs Braised with Way-Down-South Sauce

Serves 4

2 pounds country-style ribs or your favorite ribs

2 shallots, minced

6 cloves garlic, finely minced

2 tablespoons chopped fresh oregano

2 tablespoons minced fresh thyme leaves

2 cups dry red wine

1 $\frac{1}{2}$ cups ketchup

$\frac{1}{4}$ cup Worcestershire sauce

3 tablespoons brown sugar

2 tablespoons dark sesame oil

2 tablespoons chile powder

2 tablespoons molasses

1 tablespoon Tabasco sauce

1 tablespoon chile sauce

Remove the membrane from the underside of the ribs as shown on page 19.

To make the sauce, place all the sauce ingredients in a 3-quart saucepan. Bring to a low boil, cover, and reduce the heat to a simmer. Simmer for 20 minutes.

To braise the ribs, add the ribs to the sauce, cover, and maintain the ribs at a simmer. Cook the ribs until the meat is tender, about 1 hour. About every 15 minutes during cooking, stir the ribs. Temporarily remove the ribs from the pan and, using strips of paper towels, lift off all oil that is floating on the surface of the sauce. Return the ribs to the pan and bring to a simmer for 5 minutes, to heat through. If you do not plan to serve the ribs within the hour, they may be refrigerated in the sauce up to 24 hours before returning the ribs to a simmer.

If the sauce has not thickened into a glaze, temporarily remove the ribs and boil the sauce over high heat until it thickens enough to coat a spoon, about 5 minutes. Return the ribs to the pan. You can keep the ribs warm for up to 1 hour, on lowest heat, before serving. Serve the ribs glazed in the sauce.

Braised Ribs with Southwest Chile Glaze

Serves 4

4 pounds (about 2 sides) pork baby back ribs, or your favorite ribs
1/4 cup olive oil
3 cloves garlic, finely minced
3 finely minced serrano chiles, including the seeds
1 tablespoon cornstarch
3 ounces soft goat cheese, crumbled and refrigerated
1/4 cup chopped cilantro sprigs

SOUTHWEST CHILE AND TEQUILA GLAZE

2 vine-ripened tomatoes, seeded and chopped
1 cup chicken broth
1/2 cup dry white or red wine
3 tablespoons oyster sauce
1 tablespoon brown sugar
1 tablespoon ground coriander
1 teaspoon ground cumin

Ask the butcher to cut the ribs across the bone, into 2-inch-wide strips. Remove the membrane from the underside of the ribs, as shown on page 19. Then cut the strips into 6-inch lengths.

To make the glaze, combine all the glaze ingredients in a small bowl. Stir well.

To braise the ribs, place a heavy stewpot over medium heat. Add the cooking oil. When the oil gives off little wisps of smoke, add the ribs. Fry the ribs until they are lightly browned, about 5 minutes. Tip out and discard the oil. Add the garlic and chiles to the pot holding the ribs. Stir with the ribs over medium heat for 30 seconds. Then add the glaze. Bring to a low boil, cover the pot, and decrease the heat to low, so the glaze is at a simmer. Cook the ribs until the meat is tender, about 1 hour. About every 15 minutes during cooking, stir the ribs.

Temporarily remove the ribs from the pot and, using strips of paper towels, lift off all oil that is floating on the surface of the glaze. Return the ribs to the pot and bring to a simmer for 5 minutes, to heat through. If you do not plan to serve the ribs within the hour, they may be refrigerated in the sauce up to 24 hours before returning the ribs to a simmer.

Mix the cornstarch with an equal amount of cold water. Stir in just enough of the cornstarch mixture to lightly thicken the sauce. You can keep the ribs warm for up to 1 hour, on lowest heat, before serving. When serving, sprinkle the goat cheese and cilantro over the ribs.

Ribs Simmered in Thai Green Curry Paste

Serves 4

4 pounds (about 2 sides) spareribs, or your favorite ribs

1 cup chicken broth

1 cup coconut milk, unsweetened

3 tablespoons Thai or Vietnamese fish sauce

$1/4$ cup flavorless cooking oil

1 tablespoon cornstarch

THAI GREEN CURRY PASTE

4 whole cloves

12 black peppercorns

2 teaspoons coriander seeds

1 teaspoon caraway seeds

$1/2$ teaspoon cumin seeds

6 cloves garlic, peeled

1 medium shallot, peeled

3 whole serrano chiles, stemmed

$3/4$ cup fresh basil leaves

$3/4$ cup fresh cilantro sprigs

1 teaspoon salt

$1/2$ cup flavorless cooking oil

Ask the butcher to cut the ribs across the bone, into 2-inch-wide lengths. Remove the membrane from the underside of the ribs, as shown on page 19. Then cut the ribs into 6-inch lengths. Combine the broth, coconut milk, and fish sauce and set aside.

To make the green curry paste, place the cloves, peppercorns, and coriander, caraway, and cumin seeds in a small frying pan with no oil. Place the pan over medium heat and cook until the spices just begin to smoke, about 1 minute. Then, in an electric spice grinder, grind the spices into a powder. In a food processor, mince the garlic, shallot, and chiles. Remove the processor top and add the basil, cilantro, and salt. Then mince very finely. Add the ground spices and mince again. Now, with the machine running, slowly pour the cooking oil down the feed tube and mince until a paste is formed. Transfer to a small bowl.

To braise the ribs, place a heavy stewpot over medium heat. Add the cooking oil. When the oil gives off little wisps of smoke, add the ribs. Fry the ribs until they are lightly browned, about 5 minutes. Tip out and discard the oil. Add the curry paste to the pot holding the ribs and stir over medium heat for 30 seconds. Then add the coconut milk mixture. Bring to a low boil, cover the pot, and reduce the heat to low, so the sauce is at a simmer. Cook the ribs until the meat is tender, about 1 hour. About every 15 minutes during cooking, stir the ribs.

Temporarily remove the ribs from the pot and, using strips of paper towels, lift off all oil that is floating on the surface of the sauce. Return the ribs to the pot and bring to a simmer for 5 minutes, to heat through. If you do not plan to serve the ribs within the hour, they may be refrigerated in the sauce for up to 24 hours before returning the ribs to a simmer.

Mix the cornstarch with an equal amount of cold water. Stir in just enough of the cornstarch mixture to lightly thicken the sauce. You can keep the ribs warm for up to 1 hour, on lowest heat, before serving. Serve the ribs glazed in the sauce.

Acknowledgments

Many friends helped bring this book into print, and we deeply appreciate their support. Thank you Ten Speed Press, particularly Phil Wood, our publisher, and Dennis Hayes in special sales, who urged us to do this book. Many thanks also to our editor, Jason Rath, and to executive editor Lorena Jones, who oversaw the entire project. Our friend and book designer Beverly Wilson contributed her unique vision for the book. Jack and Dolores Cakebread provided their winery kitchen for testing many of these recipes with a small group of cooking friends. All the recipes were developed using the superb Viking Range equipment and Calphalon Cookware. A special thank-you to George Schamun, head of the meat department at Vallerga's Market, for providing all the great ribs for recipe testing and photography.

Artists' Credits

We'd like to give special thanks to the incredibly talented and innovative ceramic artist Julie Sanders of the Cyclamen Collection, Emeryville, Calif., for her platters, plates, and bowls, which add so much color to the photographs on pages 55, 65, 73, 77, 83, 91, 105, 115, and 131.

Thank you also to Vanderbilt & Co., St. Helena, Calif., for the pig sculpture on page 1. Tantau Gallery, St. Helena, Calif., provided the Heritage Toy music box from Sebec, Maine, on page 4, and the Barbara Eigen plate on page 141. Thanks to Aubergine Gallery, Corte Madera, Calif., for the Italian tableware on page 97.

ZIA Houseworks, Berkeley, Calif., was the source for the Kathy Erteman platter on page 101. The Salon at Auberge du Soleil, Rutherford, Calif., provided the glass platter on page 128. The Valley Exchange and the Culinary Institute of America at Greystone, both in St. Helena, Calif., provided the wooden cow on page 158, and the "chef" on page 151. Thank you all.

Conversion Charts

Liquid Measurements

Cups and Spoons	Liquid Ounces	Approximate Metric Term
1 tsp	$^1/_6$ oz	*
1 Tb	$^1/_2$ oz	*
$^1/_4$ c	2 oz	$^1/_2$ dL
$^1/_3$ c	2 $^2/_3$ oz	$^3/_4$ dL
$^1/_2$ c	4 oz	1 dL
$^2/_3$ c	5 $^1/_3$ oz	1 $^1/_2$ dL
$^3/_4$ c	6 oz	1 $^3/_4$ dL
1 c	8 oz	$^1/_4$ L
1 $^1/_4$ c	10 oz	3 dL
1 $^1/_3$ c	10 $^2/_3$ oz	3 $^1/_4$ dL
1 $^1/_2$ c	12 oz	3 $^1/_2$ dL
1 $^2/_3$ c	13 $^1/_3$ oz	3 $^3/_4$ dL
1 $^3/_4$ c	14 oz	4 dL
2c; 1 pt	16 oz	$^1/_2$ L
2 $^1/_2$ c	20 oz	6 dL
3 c	24 oz	$^3/_4$ L
3 $^1/_2$ c	28 oz	$^4/_5$ L
4 c	32 oz	1 L
5 c	40 oz	1 $^1/_4$ L
6 c	48 oz	1 $^1/_2$ L
8 c	64 oz	2 L
10 c	80 oz	2 $^1/_2$ L
12 c	96 oz	2 $^3/_4$ L
4 qt	128 oz	3 $^3/_4$ L

* Metric equivalent too small for home measure.

Temperatures

275°F = 140°C
300°F = 150°C
325°F = 170°C
350°F = 180°C
375°F = 190°C
400°F = 200°C
425°F = 215°C
450°F = 230°C
475°F = 240°C
500°F = 250°C

Length

$^1/_8$ in = 3 mm
$^1/_4$ in = 6 mm
$^1/_3$ in = 1 cm
$^1/_2$ in = 1.5 cm
$^3/_4$ in = 2 cm
1 in = 2$^1/_2$ cm
1$^1/_2$ in = 4 cm
2 in = 5 cm
2$^1/_2$ in = 6 cm
4 in = 10 cm
8 in = 20 cm
10 in = 25 cm

Other Conversions

Ounces to milliliters: multiply ounces by 29.57
Quarts to liters: multiply quarts by 0.95
Milliliters to ounces: multiply milliliters by 0.034
Liters to quarts: multiply liters by 1.057
Ounces to grams: multiply ounces by 28.3
Grams to ounces: multiply grams by 0.0353
Pounds to grams: multiply pounds by 453.59
Pounds to kilograms: multiply pounds by 0.45
Cups to liters: multiply cups by 0.24

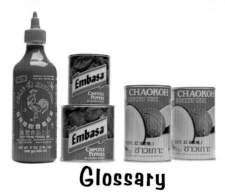

Glossary

Chiles, Ancho: These reddish-purple dried chiles have a fruity, mildly spicy taste that makes them a great addition to barbecue sauces. They are sold in all Mexican markets and American supermarkets that have a wide selection of dry chiles. Substitute: mulato or pasilla.

Chiles, fresh: The smaller the chile, the spicier its taste. Over 80 percent of the "heat" is concentrated in the inside ribbing and seeds. Because it is a tedious operation to remove the seeds from Scotch bonnet, jalapeño, and serrano chiles, we always mince the chiles including their seeds. If recipes specify seeding a small chile, just use half the amount of chiles and mince the chiles including their seeds in an electric mini-chopper. Substitute: your favorite bottled chile sauce. (See photo of serrano chiles, page 98, top.)

Chile Sauces: These are sauces whose primary ingredient is chiles, and are not to be confused with tomato-based "chile sauces." There are countless varieties of chile sauces. Use your own favorite chile sauce, added to provide "heat" to the food, and vary the amount depending on personal preference. Most of the recipes designate "Asian chile sauce." Best brand: Rooster Brand Delicious Hot Chili Garlic Sauce, sold in 8-ounce clear plastic bottles with a green cap. Refrigerate after opening. Substitute: One or more fresh jalapeño or serrano chiles.

Chipotle Chiles in Adobo Sauce: Having a spicy, deep-smoky flavor, these are smoked, dried jalapeños (chipotle chiles) that are stewed in a tomato-vinegar-garlic sauce (adobo sauce). Chipotle chiles in adobo sauce are available in 4-ounce cans at all Mexican markets and many supermarkets. To use, purée the chiles with the adobo sauce in an electric mini-chopper. It is unnecessary to remove the seeds. Substitute: none. See photo page 86, botttom.)

Citrus Juice and Zest: Freshly squeezed citrus juice has a sparkling taste completely absent in all store-bought juices. Because juice's flavor deteriorates quickly, always squeeze citrus juice within hours of use and keep it refrigerated. Recipes that say "finely minced zest" mean to remove the colored skin of citrus using a simple tool called a "zester" and then finely mince the zest rather than scraping the citrus against the fine mesh of a cheese grater, which is very time-consuming.

Coconut Milk: Adds flavor and body to sauces. Always purchase a Thai brand whose ingredients are just coconut and water. Do not buy the new "low calorie" coconut milk, which has a terrible taste. Stir the coconut milk before using. Best brand: Chaokoh Brand from Thailand. Once opened, store coconut milk in the refrigerator for up to one week, then discard. Substitute: Use half-and-half.

Cooking Oil: Use any tasteless oil that has a high smoking temperature, such as peanut oil, canola oil, safflower oil, or corn oil.

Fish Sauce, Thai: Fish sauce, made from fermenting fish in brine, is used in Southeast Asian cooking in much the same way that the Chinese use soy sauce. Purchase Thai or Vietnamese fish sauce, which has the lowest salt content. Best brands: Three Crab Brand, Phu Quoc Flying Lion Brand, or Tiparos Brand Fish Sauce. Substitute: thin soy sauce (although the flavor is quite different).

Five-Spice Powder: This is a blend of anise, fennel, cinnamon, cloves, and Szechuan pepper. It is sold at all Asian markets and in the spice section of most supermarkets.

Ginger Root, fresh: These pungent and spicy "roots," grown in Hawaii, are available at all supermarkets in the produce section. Buy firm ginger with a smooth skin. Don't peel ginger unless the skin is wrinkled. Because the tough ginger fiber runs lengthwise along the root, always cut the ginger crosswise, in paper-thin slices. Then very finely mince it in an electric mini-chopper. Store in the refrigerator or at room temperature for up to one month. There is no substitute for fresh ginger. (See photo page 116, bottom.)

Herbs, Fresh and Dried: Fresh herbs have a far more complex flavor than their dried counterparts. The only time we use dried herbs is when they are included in dry rubs. If you cannot find the fresh herb specified, substitute another fresh herb.

Hoisin Sauce: Hoisin sauce, a thick, sweet, and spicy dark condiment, is made with soy beans, chiles, garlic, ginger, and sugar. Once opened, it keeps indefinitely at room temperature. Best brand: Koon Chun Hoisin Sauce.

Lemongrass: Available in most Asian markets, this is one of the most widely used herbs in Southeast Asia. However, the lemongrass sold in markets already has the extremely fragrant green leaves cut off, and the stems are tough and flavorless. Since a lemongrass stalk will develop roots when placed in water or potting soil, grow your own. For cooking, use just the leaves, very finely minced. The flavor is not quite the same, but as a substitute use 1 tablespoon grated lemon skin.

Mustards; Dijon, Creole, Honey: All types of mustard pastes can been used interchangeably. For Dijon mustard, we prefer Maille brand, and for Creole mustard, Zatarain's.

Olive Oil: Recipes specifying "extra virgin olive oil" benefit from this intensely flavored green-tinted oil to add additional flavor. Recipes specifying just "olive oil" use a lighter-colored oil when little or no olive oil taste is wanted in the dish.

Oyster Sauce: Also called "oyster flavored sauce," this gives dishes a rich taste without a hint of its seafood origins. Keeps indefinitely in the refrigerator. There is no substitute. Although it is available at every supermarket, the following best brands are available mostly at Asian markets: Sa Cheng Oyster Flavored Sauce, Hop Sing Lung Oyster Sauce, and Lee Kum Kee Oyster Flavored Sauce, Premium Brand.

Plum Sauce: This chutney-like condiment is made with plums, apricots, garlic, red chiles, sugar, vinegar, salt, and water. It is available canned or bottled at all Asian markets and most supermarkets. Best brand: Koon Chun. It will keep indefinitely if stored in the refrigerator.

Pomegranate Molasses (Pomegranate Concentrate Juice): Much used in the Middle East, this is a thick, very dark syrup, with a strong fruity taste. Look for this in Middle Eastern markets and gourmet products shops. Although the flavor is not the same, substitute an equal amount of dark corn syrup and grape jelly.

Powders, Garlic and Onion: These are dehydrated garlic or onion flakes that are powdered. Their strong, sharp taste makes them appropiate to use only in dry rub mixes, and only in small amounts. If you substitute garlic or onion powder for the fresh garlic or onion used in any of the marinades or sauces, the taste of the dish will be ruined.

Red Peppers, Roasted: These are sweet red bell peppers that are roasted, and then peeled and seeded. While they are best tasting when roasted fresh over a gas stovetop flame or under an electric oven broiler, very good tasting roasted red peppers are sold in jars by most supermarkets. Available in 6-, 8-, and 15-ounce bottles, and sold alongside pickles and relishes, the roasted red peppers are submerged in water and citric acid. Once opened, they will last indefinitely if kept refrigerated.

Rice Wine and Dry Sherry: We prefer the flavor of Chinese rice wine. Use a good-quality Chinese rice wine or an American or Spanish dry sherry. For rice wine, the best brands are Pagoda Brand Shao Xing Rice Wine, Pagoda Brand Shao Hsing Hua Tiao Chiew, or use a moderately expensive dry sherry. You can substitute dry Japanese sake or dry vermouth, but not Mirin, which is a sweet Japanese cooking wine.

Salt, Kosher: This coarse sea salt has a wonderful natural salt flavor that is far superior to table salt. Used by all chefs, if you substitute kosher salt for regular salt or the expensive "gourmet" sea salt, you will need to use a little bit more.

Sesame Oil, Dark: A nutty, dark golden brown oil made from toasted crushed sesame seeds, do not confuse dark sesame oil with the American manufactured clear colored and tasteless sesame oil or Chinese black sesame oil, which has a strong unpleasant taste. Dark sesame oil will last for at least a year at room temperature and indefinitely in the refrigerator. Best brand: Kadoya Sesame Oil.

Soy Sauce, Dark: "Dark," "heavy," or "black" soy sauce is "thin soy sauce" with the addition of molasses. It is used to add a rich flavor and color to sauces, stews, and soups. Never confuse "dark" soy sauce with "thick" soy sauce, which has a syrup-like consistency and an unpleasantly strong taste. Once opened, dark soy sauce keeps indefinitely at room temperature. Best brand: Pearl River Bridge Brand Mushroom Soy Sauce.

Soy Sauce, Thin: "Thin" or "light" soy sauce is a watery, mildly salty liquid made from soybeans, roasted wheat, yeast, and salt. If you are concerned about sodium, reduce the quantity of soy sauce, rather than using the inferior tasting, more expensive low-sodium brands. Best brands: Pearl River Bridge Brand Golden Label Superior Soy Sauce, Koon Chun Brand Thin Soy Sauce, or Kikkoman Regular Soy Sauce.

Spices: For convenience, most of us use preground spices. However, the flavor will be greatly improved if you grind the whole spices into a powder by using an electric spice grinder. Store spices in a cool, dark pantry. Discard whole spices after 2 years and ground spices after 1 year.

Vinegars: In recipes that use a certain type of wine vinegar, you can use any type of wine vinegar. In recipes that call for cider vinegar or white distilled vinegar, you can use these interchangably, or substitue white wine vinegar. For recipes using balsamic vinegar, make the effort to purchase this uniquely flavored nutty, mildly sour, and slightly sweet-tasting vinegar. Use a moderately priced balsamic vinegar ($5 for an 8-ounce bottle) available in most supermarkets. If using the mild-tasting Japanese rice vinegar, avoid "seasoned" or "gourmet" rice vinegar, which has sugar and MSG added.

Worcestershire Sauce: This sauce, which was originally developed by the English in India, contains soy sauce, garlic, tamarind, onions, molasses, lime, anchovies, vinegar, and seasonings. We prefer Lea & Perrins. As a substitute, use dark soy sauce.

Index

A

All-Purpose Dry Rub, 58
Amazing Ribs with Amazing Glaze, 74
Ancho chiles
    Ancho Chile–Glazed Ribs, 80
    Ribs with Ancho Marmalade Rub,
      122–123
    Ribs with Oaxacan Mole Sauce, 81–82
    Southwest Barbecued Ribs, 90
    Southwest Chile Barbecued Ribs,
      88–89
    Spareribs with Cowboy Rub, 70–71
Apricot Glaze, Ribs Crusted with, 114
Asian Cabernet Sauce, 138–139
Asian Pesto, 48–49

B

Baby back ribs (pork), 11
    Best Chinese Baby Back Ribs, 36
    Braised Ribs in Chinese Black Bean
      Sauce, 142–143
    Braised Ribs with Southwest Chile
      Glaze, 147
    Carolina Barbecued Ribs, 68
    Mahogany Glazed Ribs, 38–39
    New Orleans–Style Glazed Ribs, 144
    Pork Baby Back Ribs with Jamaican
      Jerk Marinade, 102
    Pork Baby Back Ribs with Spicy Asian
      Chipotle Chile Sauce, 67
    Pork Baby Back Ribs with Spicy Peanut
      Butter Slather, 50
    Ribs Braised with Soy and Ginger, 136
    Ribs in Spicy Coconut Herb Sauce, 140
    Ribs with Ancho Marmalade Rub,
      122–123
    Southwest Chile Barbecued Ribs,
      88–89
    Spicy Cherry-Glazed Ribs, 120
    Thai Baby Back Ribs, 42
Balsamic Vinegar, Soy, and Honey
    Mustard Ribs, 108
Basting, 20
Beef back ribs, 13
    Amazing Ribs with Amazing Glaze, 74
    Chipotle-Coriander Cured Ribs, 93
    Crushed Peppercorn and Orange
      Glazed Ribs, 76
    Ribs Marinated with Molasses-Chile
      Barbecue Sauce, 75
    Ribs with Fiery Mango Marinade, 128
    Sweet-and-Sour Fiery Ribs, 84–85
    Sweet and Spicy Southern Tomato-
      Glazed Ribs, 60–61
Beef short ribs
    about, 14
    Ribs with Spicy Tomato Glaze, 134
Best Chinese Baby Back Ribs, 36
Black Bean Sauce, Chinese, Braised Ribs
    in, 142–143
Boar ribs, wild, 15
Boiling, 18
Braised Ribs in Chinese Black Bean
    Sauce, 142–143

Braised Ribs with Southwest Chile Glaze,
    147
Braising, 31–33, 133–149
Buffalo ribs, 15

C

Cajun Pepper Mustard-Crusted Ribs, 72
Carolina Barbecued Ribs, 68
Carolina Mountain Barbecue Sauce, 68
Cherry-Glazed Ribs, Spicy, 120
Chiles. *See also* Ancho chiles; Chipotle
    chiles
    Braised Ribs with Southwest Chile
      Glaze, 147
    Chile-Fruit Barbecue Sauce, 88–89
    Pork Baby Back Ribs with Jamaican
      Jerk Marinade, 102
    Ribs Marinated with Molasses-Chile
      Barbecue Sauce, 75
    Ribs Simmered in Thai Green Curry
      Paste, 148–149
    Ribs with Spicy Caribbean Pineapple
      Marinade, 130
    Rosemary, Chile, and Hoisin Ribs,
      98–99
    Southwest Barbecued Ribs, 90
    Southwest Chile Barbecued Ribs,
      88–89
    Strawberry-Habanero Marinated Ribs,
      124
Chinese Barbecue Sauce, 36
Chinese Black Bean Sauce, 142–143
Chipotle chiles
    Chipotle-Coriander Cured Ribs, 93
    Chipotle-Honey Barbecue Sauce,
      86–87
    Pork Baby Back Ribs with Spicy Asian
      Chipotle Chile Sauce, 67
    Ribs Rubbed with Secret Chipotle-
      Honey Barbecue Sauce, 86–87
    Ribs with Fiery Mango Marinade, 128
    Spareribs with Cowboy Rub, 70–71
    Sweet-and-Sour Fiery Ribs, 84–85
Coconut
    Ribs in Spicy Coconut Herb Sauce, 140
    Ribs Simmered in Thai Green Curry
      Paste, 148–149
Cooking techniques
    basting, 20
    boiling, 18
    braising, 31–33
    with brown paper bag, 21
    combination, 33
    cutting, 21–22
    grilling, 22–26
    marinating, 20
    oven roasting, 29–31
    removing the membrane, 19
    smoking, 27–29
Country-style spareribs, 12
    Ribs Braised with Way-Down-South
      Sauce, 146
    Ribs Simmered in Asian Cabernet
      Sauce, 138–139

Ribs with All-Purpose Dry Rub and
  Sweet-and-Sour Mop, 58
Ribs with Oaxacan Mole Sauce, 81–82
Spicy Honey Mustard Ribs, 106–107
Spicy Pirate Ribs with Lemon Mop, 66
Cowboy Rub, 70–71
Crushed Peppercorn and Orange Glazed
  Ribs, 76
Curries
  Ribs Simmered in Thai Green Curry
    Paste, 148–149
  Ribs with Thai Red Curry Sauce,
    40–41
  Thai Green Curry Ribs, 52–53
Cutting, 21–22

E
East-West Lemon-Glazed Ribs, 103
Elk ribs, 15
Exotic ribs, 15

F
Fiery Mango Marinade, 128
Fiery Sauce, 84–85
Fig Glaze, Spicy, Ribs with, 126–127
Frozen ribs, 18

G
Green Curry Rub, 52–53
Grilling, 22–26

H
Hoisin–Peanut Butter Rub, 45

J
Jerk Marinade, 102

L
Lamb ribs
  about, 15
  Spicy Orange-Glazed Ribs, 118
Lemons
  East-West Lemon-Glazed Ribs, 103
  Lemon-Honey Glaze, 44
  Moroccan Glazed Ribs, 104
  Spicy Lemon Mop, 66
  Tuscan-Style Barbecued Ribs, 110
Louisiana Marinade, 62–63

M
Mahogany Glazed Ribs, 38–39
Mangoes
  Ribs with Fiery Mango Marinade, 128
  Ribs with Thai Mango Sauce, 121
  Southwest Chile Barbecued Ribs,
    88–89
Marinating, 20
Membrane, removing the, 19
Middle Eastern Ribs with Spicy
  Pomegranate Glaze, 100
Molasses-Chile Barbecue Sauce, 75
Moroccan Glazed Ribs, 104
Mushrooms

Ribs Simmered in Asian Cabernet
  Sauce, 138–139
Spicy Braised Spareribs, 137
Mustard, Garlic, and Rosemary Marinade,
  96
Mustard, Soy, and Juniper Berry Rub, 64

N
New Orleans–Style Glazed Ribs, 144

O
Oaxacan Mole Sauce, 81–82
Oranges
  Crushed Peppercorn and Orange
    Glazed Ribs, 76
  Ribs Rubbed with Asian Pesto, 48–49
  Ribs with Ancho Marmalade Rub,
    122–123
  Ribs with Spicy Fig Glaze, 126–127
  Southwest Barbecued Ribs, 90
  Southwest Chile Barbecued Ribs,
    88–89
  Spicy Orange-Glazed Ribs, 118
Oven roasting, 29–31

P
Peanut butter
  Pork Baby Back Ribs with Spicy Peanut
    Butter Slather, 50
  Spareribs with Hoisin–Peanut Butter
    Rub, 45
Pesto, Asian, 48–49
Pineapple Marinade, Spicy Caribbean,
  Ribs with, 130
Pomegranate Glaze, Spicy, Middle Eastern
  Ribs with, 100
Pork. See Baby back ribs; Country-style
  spareribs; Spareribs

R
Raspberry-Glazed Ribs, Sweet-and-Sour,
  116–117
Red Curry Sauce, 40–41
Ribs Braised with Soy and Ginger, 136
Ribs Braised with Way-Down-South
  Sauce, 146
Ribs Crusted with Apricot Glaze, 114
Ribs in Spicy Coconut Herb Sauce, 140
Ribs Louisiana Style, 62–63
Ribs Marinated with Molasses-Chile
  Barbecue Sauce, 75
Ribs Rubbed with Asian Pesto, 48–49
Ribs Rubbed with Secret Chipotle-Honey
  Barbecue Sauce, 86–87
Ribs Simmered in Asian Cabernet Sauce,
  138–139
Ribs Simmered in Thai Green Curry
  Paste, 148–149
Ribs with All-Purpose Dry Rub and Sweet
  and-Sour Mop, 58
Ribs with Ancho Marmalade Rub,
  122–123
Ribs with Fiery Mango Marinade, 128
Ribs with Oaxacan Mole Sauce, 81–82

Ribs with Spicy Caribbean Pineapple
    Marinade, 130
Ribs with Spicy Fig Glaze, 126–127
Ribs with Spicy Tomato Glaze, 134
Ribs with Thai Mango Sauce, 121
Ribs with Thai Red Curry Sauce, 40–41
Rosemary, Chile, and Hoisin Ribs, 98–99

S

Smoking, 27–29
Southern Tomato Glaze, 60–61
Southwest Barbecued Ribs, 90
Southwest Chile Barbecued Ribs, 88–89
Southwest Chile Glaze, 147
Soy-Ginger Braising Sauce, 136
Spareribs, 10. *See also* Country-style
    spareribs
    Ancho Chile–Glazed Ribs, 80
    Balsamic Vinegar, Soy, and Honey
        Mustard Ribs, 108
    Cajun Pepper Mustard-Crusted Ribs,
        72
    East-West Lemon-Glazed Ribs, 103
    Middle Eastern Ribs with Spicy
        Pomegranate Glaze, 100
    Moroccan Glazed Ribs, 104
    Ribs Louisiana Style, 62–63
    Ribs Rubbed with Asian Pesto, 48–49
    Ribs Rubbed with Secret Chipotle-
        Honey Barbecue Sauce, 86–87
    Ribs Simmered in Thai Green Curry
        Paste, 148–149
    Ribs with Spicy Caribbean Pineapple
        Marinade, 130
    Ribs with Spicy Fig Glaze, 126–127
    Ribs with Thai Mango Sauce, 121
    Rosemary, Chile, and Hoisin Ribs,
        98–99
    Southwest Barbecued Ribs, 90
    Spareribs with Cowboy Rub, 70–71
    Spareribs with Hoisin–Peanut Butter
        Rub, 45
    Spareribs with Mustard, Garlic, and
        Rosemary Marinade, 96
    Spareribs with Mustard, Soy, and
        Juniper Berry Rub, 64
    Spicy Braised Spareribs, 137
    Spicy Ribs in Lemongrass-Honey
        Glaze, 44
    Strawberry-Habanero Marinated Ribs,
        124
    Sweet-and-Sour Raspberry-Glazed
        Ribs, 116–117
    Szechuan Fire Ribs, 46
    Tandoori Spareribs, 54
    Teriyaki Ribs, 47
    Thai Green Curry Ribs, 52–53
    Tuscan-Style Barbecued Ribs, 110
Spices, toasting, 92
Spicy Apricot Glaze, 114
Spicy Asian Chipotle Chile Sauce, 67
Spicy Braised Spareribs, 137
Spicy Caribbean Pineapple Marinade, 130
Spicy Cherry-Glazed Ribs, 120
Spicy Coconut Herb Sauce, 140

Spicy Fig Glaze, 126–127
Spicy Honey Mustard Ribs, 106–107
Spicy Lemon Mop, 66
Spicy New Orleans–Style Sauce, 144
Spicy Orange-Glazed Ribs, 118
Spicy Peanut Butter Marinade, 50
Spicy Pirate Ribs with Lemon Mop, 66
Spicy Pomegranate Glaze, 100
Spicy Ribs in Lemongrass-Honey Glaze,
    44
Spicy Tomato Glaze, 134
Strawberry-Habanero Marinated Ribs, 124
Sweet-and-Sour Fiery Ribs, 84–85
Sweet-and-Sour Mop, 58
Sweet-and-Sour Raspberry-Glazed Ribs,
    116–117
Sweet and Spicy Southern Tomato-Glazed
    Ribs, 60–61
Sweet Nutmeg Dry Rub, 120
Szechuan Fire Ribs, 46

T

Tandoori Spareribs, 54
Teriyaki Ribs, 47
Thai Baby Back Ribs, 42
Thai Barbecue Sauce, 42
Thai Green Curry Paste, 148–149
Thai Green Curry Ribs, 52–53
Thai Mango Sauce, 121
Tomatoes
    Braised Ribs with Southwest Chile
        Glaze, 147
    New Orleans–Style Glazed Ribs, 144
    Ribs Louisiana Style, 62–63
    Ribs Rubbed with Secret Chipotle-
        Honey Barbecue Sauce, 86–87
    Ribs with Oaxacan Mole Sauce, 81–82
    Ribs with Spicy Tomato Glaze, 134
    Ribs with Thai Red Curry Sauce,
        40–41
    Southwest Chile Barbecued Ribs,
        88–89
    Spicy Braised Spareribs, 137
    Sweet-and-Sour Fiery Ribs, 84–85
    Sweet and Spicy Southern Tomato-
        Glazed Ribs, 60–61
Tuscan Marinade, 110
Tuscan-Style Barbecued Ribs, 110

V .

Venison ribs, 15

W

Way-Down-South Sauce, 146

About the Authors

The husband-and-wife team of Hugh Carpenter and Teri Sandison are the authors of *Hot Wok; Hot Chicken; Hot Pasta; Hot Barbecue; Hot Vegetables;* the *Fusion Food Cookbook,* which received a James Beard Award nomination in 1995; *Chopstix*, which received the IACP nomination for Best Food Photography in 1990; and *Pacific Flavors*, which won the IACP award for Best Asian Food Cookbook in 1988 and the Who's Who of Cooking Platinum Plate Award for Best Food Photography in 1989.

Hugh Carpenter is one of America's most popular cooking teachers and writers, and his articles appear in many newspapers and magazines. In addition to the cooks he has influenced through frequent television and radio appearances, he has taught more than 70,000 students in classes at cooking schools throughout North America and at his own school in Napa Valley, California, which he runs in association with the Cakebread Winery.

Teri Sandison began her art career in painting and drawing. She then studied photography at Art Center College of Design, where she specialized in food and wine photography and later was a member of the photography faculty for more than three years. She has done the photography for more than 40 cookbooks from leading publishers and has clients who come from across the United States to her St. Helena photography studio. Since 1995, she has been adjunct instructor in food photography and food styling at the Culinary Institute of America, Greystone campus.

Teri and Hugh live in the Napa Valley community of Oakville.

Other Cookbooks from Hugh Carpenter & Teri Sandison

Fifty bold and sophisticated yet easy stir-fry recipes seasoned with a host of exciting ingredients. Perfect ideas for fresh, healthy weeknight meals or weekend entertaining. Includes more than fifty vibrant color photos.

Fifty wild and zesty recipes that combine chicken with the distinct flavors and cuisines of the world. Discover delicious and elegant ways to serve one of the most versatile and healthy meats. More than fifty color photos provide dramatic presentation ideas

Fifty fresh and sensational recipes that take pasta to new and dazzling heights. Packed with easy, inventive ideas, this is the complete resource for busy cooks at all levels of experience. Includes more than fifty exciting color photos.

Fifty sizzling recipes for classic barbecue favorites and innovative grilled food from around the world. From simple any-night delights to elaborate weekend feasts, this tantalizing offering in the ever-popular *Hot* series will heat up backyards and kitchens alike.

Fifty delicious and healthful recipes that will enchant vegetable lovers everywhere. These easy-to-prepare but stunning dishes use fresh vegetables ranging from artichokes to zucchini. With beautiful photos and creative serving suggestions, this book is certain to impress and inspire.